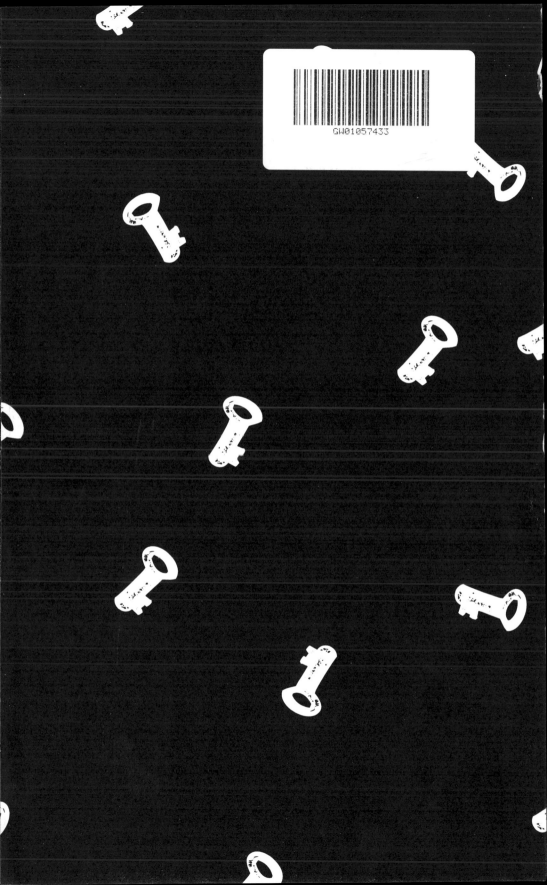

GW01057433

# IRAN

## DEMOCRACY WITHIN OUR REACH

**Behrooz Behbudi**

# IRAN
## DEMOCRACY WITHIN OUR REACH
### Behrooz Behbudi

First Edition: June 2012

Design and Printing by Satrap Publishing (London)

Cover Illustration by Bahman Forsi

ISBN: 978–1–872302–13–3

Price: £9.99 – $13.99

**Satrap Publishing**

271 King Street, London W6 9LZ
Tel: 0044 20 8748 9397
Email: satrap@btconnect.com
Website: www.satrap.co.uk

For Lord Shukh
with my best
wishes

Behrooz
Behleh
June 21, 2012

To my daughter,
Elizabeth Olivia Forough - Williams Behbudi,
my son
Noah Thomas Abbas - Williams Behbudi
and their mother
Susan Maria Williams

# Contents

# Foreword

Although the notion of democracy and democratic government dates back many centuries, it has always been a chimera for Iran and the Iranian people.

The history of Iran is intertwined with the reality of despotism of many of its rulers, a disease that has become so chronic that even the people have acquired its undesirable characteristics.

Iran has also experienced religious dictatorship in its long history. However, the present religious tyranny that scars Iran has superseded all of them put together in terms of the atrocities that it has committed.

To start with, the damage that this "religious government" has done to the very sincere religious beliefs of the Iranian people is incalculable.

Today, religion and religious values in Iran are on their deathbed as a result of the acts of a group of "religious leaders" whose lust for power and plundered wealth have driven an ancient country and its people to the brink of total ruin.

There are still some people within this regime who wishfully think that they can reform it and bring prosperity and peace to our country. All they can do is to extend the parasitic life of a regime that is inherently corrupt, despotic and destructive.

Constantly at war with the Iranian people's aspirations for democracy, engaging in ideological disputes with Iran's neighbours and defying every international diplomatic norm, the Islamic Republic has tied its survival to the very existence of Iran as a nation.

Facing this gradual death of Iran at the hands of a medieval and tyrannical clique of greedy and unaccountable rulers, no Iranian patriot can remain indifferent.

Just like a great many of my compatriots whose hearts beat for the freedom and prosperity of our motherland, I have been doing my share of liberating our country from the claws of its ruling regime.

Accordingly, I have written articles in many Iranian and Western publications, given interviews to the international media, met with foreign politicians and intellectuals, invited Iranian opposition activists to attend seminars to discuss ways of uniting them under one banner for the sake of the future of Iran and whatever else that I can possibly do to help my people in their struggle to achieve freedom and human rights under a secular system of government.

I have absolutely no doubt that the love of Iran and the sacrifices that its people are making, inside and outside the country; will soon result in realising this noble dream.

This book is a reflection of my thoughts, hopes and experiences of the last several years as an active member of the freedom movement of the Iranian people.

In the first chapter, I have given a brief history of my family background and my childhood years in pre-revolutionary Iran. It is only a brief history as my objective here has not been to write an autobiography. I have only provided the reader with my family background and why I have been drawn into Iran's democracy movement.

Although my parents and grandparents came from affluent and prominent families who held high social and influential positions, this has never led me to live off their reputations or just rely on their assets and I have always worked hard to achieve my own goals in life.

The second part of the book is a collection of my interviews with the Centre for Research and Studies of Iran on various social, cultural and political issues concerning recent events in Iran.

I quite like this part of my book as the interviews gave me the chance to talk about the problems that Iran is facing today and how they can be resolved, particularly in the area of culture.

I must confess that I am not an expert on cultural issues, but having closely followed the deep cultural changes taking place in Iran in recent years; I hope I have been able to shed some light on the significant role that Culture can play in achieving democracy in a society like Iran's.

My two long interviews with the Persian language London-based Kayhan weekly complement my views in this respect.

The final part of the book consists of my articles that I have published in various Iranian papers and websites, which help the reader to get to know my thoughts and ideas even better. As these articles have been written and published for various publications and at different time, parts of them may sound repetitive and for this I apologise to the reader. I hope that in my next book in Farsi and English I will be able to publish all my future articles under a single title.

I would sincerely like to thank all my close friends and associates and all the people who have diligently helped in the publication of this book.

My particular thanks go to Dr. Ali Reza Nourizadeh, the director of the Centre for Iranian and Arab Studies and Nasser Mohammadi, the deputy editor of the Kayhan of London newspaper who have given me such valuable advice and help.

Finally, I eagerly look forward to receiving readers' comments and suggestions so that I can use them to improve my next book.

**Behrooz Behbudi**
June 2012

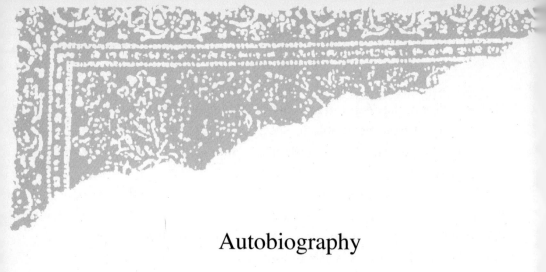

# Autobiography

The searing heat was unbearable. Tehran still did not have modern air conditioning facilities but the pure natural hot weather of those days was far cleaner than today's polluted air. In those days the weather was pleasant and temperate and the very idea of using air conditioning would have been tantamount to "pollution".

Nightfall would bring a fresh breeze that would make the traditional sleep of the families on the rooftops of their apartments both relaxing and still memorable to this day.

The moment the parents unfolded and prepared the beds inside the linen tents for their children to lie on them was probably the sweetest part of our dreams. However, in that summer, my parents could not sleep well as I had come into this world in the heat of the months of Mordad (August). Being the first child of the family, and 'more importantly', being a boy, it was only too natural for them to stay up all night to look after the first fruit of their marriage.

In those days my entire family used to live in a villa near Manzariyeh, which to this date still remains a district in north Tehran. The most developed part of it was the Manzariyeh Gardens, which had been built during the time of Nasserudin Shah of the Qajar dynasty.

Then it used to be called Hesamabad, named after an army general who had designed the building. However, before he could finish the building, Kamran Mirza, the younger brother of Muzaffaredin Shah bought the property for himself.

The ownership of the Manzariyeh Gardens changed many hands until finally it became the property of the Royal Lands during the rule of Reza Shah Pahlavi. Later, during the kingdom of Mohammad Reza Shah Pahlavi, it was donated to Iran's Scouting Organisation.

Nowadays, after the Islamic Revolution, it has been renamed as the Bahonar Camp!

Today, after this long history of changes in names and ownership, with the latest being so distasteful, I am not entirely sure if there is anything left of the delph-like atmosphere of the Manzariyeh Gardens, where the history and memoirs of the Behbudi family are written on the leaves of its mystic trees.

The only image of those heavenly Gardens in my mind is limited to a few photographs that I took during my trips there many years ago. In my trips to Iran I had gone to visit Manzariyeh to find myself and my roots again, in the sad and happy moments of my childhood. To visit a place where my mother cried in joy when I learnt to stand and walk. Then when I fell, she ran towards me and hugged me to make sure I was safe.

I can still remember how under the shadows of an old tree, I used to play with my cousins Saeed and Amir Hussein Falah and sing and then get cross with each other and ask my mother to reconcile us. Mother not only taught us to be kind to each other, but also how to love our fellow human beings. If I am filled with love for Iran today, I owe it all to my mother's teachings, who like all Iranian mothers, taught us that Life is all about sharing and loving.

Finally, after nine long months, the Behbudi family's wait ended when I was born on 31 July 1949, which was the Year of the Cow. My father was overwhelmed with joy to have a boy as his first offspring, which the elders of the family regarded as the Jewel in the Crown. Although my father was an educated intellectual, nevertheless he had grown up in a traditional family who were adamant that having a son, as one's first child, was a good omen and would secure the family's continuation.

Later, a relative read my horoscope, as a child born in the Year of the Cow, as "one whose preoccupation in life will be to fight for his ambitions, is a jack of all trades, who cannot live without being in love, a faithful friend, brave and adventurous, never attempt to get on his nerves".

The fortune teller had further made my father hopeful that a bright future awaited his son, even though he may have had his reservations as a wise and rational man.

When my auntie Effat gave the news of my birth to my father, he just stood silent as if he had been struck by lightning. He did not know if he should laugh or dance with joy. My auntie then hugged him and told him that the Gift of God had arrived, knowing that she would receive a traditional gift from her brother, as the bearer of good news always does.

My father then joined my mother in the delivery room where his exhausted wife and child were calmly resting after their joint and turbulent nine months journey together. How soon we humans forget the pains that our mothers go through to bring us into the world!

My father's stroking of my mother's hair assured her of his love for her and what was now their new family. My father had met my mother in Manzariyeh when she was only 14 years old and was a close friend of my auntie. She was the daughter of Haj Rahim Rokhnejad, a rich local trader. It must have been love at first sight as only a few months after meeting each other, they had married. My age difference with my mother at the time of my birth was only 15 years, a major factor for my very close relationship with my mother in the later years of my life, both when I was living with her and during my exiled life thousands of miles away from her.

People are born into this world with many blessings, good health, intelligence, supportive family and so on. I was lucky enough to have all of these to rely on from a very early age.

My father was a prominent figure at the Court of the Pahlavi dynasty as the man who managed their estates and properties. He was a patriot and loyal to the Shahs, and yet a generous and decent man and I have not come across anyone like him in my life. Despite his privileged social status, he always listened to other people's problems and tried to help them as much as he possibly could and everybody in the community respected him.

He was a towering figure in the small world of my childhood, to the extent that I used to think that he ruled the world, which bowed to his greatness. I was not alone in thinking that way, anyone who knew him closely, whether they were our neighbours or the faithful in the local mosque, regarded him as a man who believed in Humanity and the Day of Judgment.

His connections with the Royal Court had not changed his humble manners, as he knew in the bottom of his heart that this world is mortal and we are all going through a journey in life. Maybe the best description of him will be as a "popular courtier". He never saw himself as a "man in power" even though he did possess some. Even when in the later years of my life I had a better understanding of his duties and responsibilities, I still looked up to him as my mentor in life.

My childhood was mainly spent in a house that my father built in Behbudi alley in the Polle Choobi area of Tehran. The design of the house was a cross between modern European and traditional Iranian architecture. It was the house I grew up in with so many fond memories. The house, which witnessed my moments of sadness and happiness, now only lives in my imagination, as it was bulldozed many years ago.

It had a very large yard, in the middle, where the children would run around a little fountain and play, whilst the adults would spread a rug in one corner of it and eat juicy watermelons and chat. My father had equipped it with some of the latest appliances that were available at the time.

I was the only child of my parents until I entered secondary school, when my mum gave birth to my sister Behnaz, nicknamed as Nazee, meaning a cute little girl, which was very fitting for her! She made life even sweeter for the family, even though she overshadowed me by becoming the darling of the family, hence leading to our sibling rivalry and jealousy!

We were so close to each other that I did not even want to go to school as it meant I had to leave her alone at home, a thought that really depressed me. My only consolation was that I could still play with Nazee the moment I got back from school. However, as I grew up and entered high school, the gap between me and my family became wider as my studies and teenage life turned me into an independent individual who was now involved in various social activities away from home, something that my parents did not mind.

My father enrolled me at Brazil School. Apparently, in Brazil, a reputable state school had been named Tehran as a gesture of good diplomatic relations between the two countries and to reciprocate this goodwill the Shah had ordered a new school to be named "Brazil" in the capital. Its building was behind the Faculty of Foundation Studies and our head teacher was Mr. Mustafa Grayeli, a highly educated, decent and smart scholar whose shoes always shone. His wife also worked at the school as the head of administration. Our teachers were from amongst the most experienced academics in the country. In those days the school had only 160 pupils, some of whom may still be alive in various corners of Iran whilst others may have left our earthly life.

However, I have no doubt that all those like me, who are still around, will remember the excitement of our break times in the school yard when we used to play and run after each other and drink our early morning milk and then have our lunch packs which were given to all school children free of charge, as part of the Shah's social and educational reform programs.

At Brazil School I joined the Scouts, which acted as a stepping stone between childhood and teenage life. I still regard my time in the Scouts as the formative years of my early life, when I learnt how to accept responsibility and carry it out in the best possible way.

If my educational ambitions were the result of my family upbringing, my managerial skills have their foundations in the discipline that I acquired during my scouting life. No wonder I soon achieved the rank of deputy corporal in the Scouts' hierarchy!

Scouting not only teaches you how best to manage your responsibilities, it also strengthens the mental process of your decision making and increases your sense of aiding your fellow human beings, the very principles that led me to establish the Council for a Democratic Iran, which seeks to help my compatriots to achieve democracy and progress for our beloved country.

All the Scouts had to wear a sky blue uniform that is the symbol of love and life. In this uniform, all class barriers gave way to a unity of purpose amongst everyone. One of the many important values that Scouting taught me was a sense of patriotism. Every single day at the camps we would stand at attention in front of Iran's flag and pledge our loyalty and allegiance to the proud and ancient symbol that many great patriots had fought and died for over the course of a very long history.

My hard work and discipline at primary school managed to get me a place at Alborz College. It was only a stone throw away from where we lived and was different from the primary school in many respects. At Alborz, everyone, from the head teacher down to the tutors, was highly strict and very disciplined. The college head teacher was Dr. Mojtahedi and Messrs Mokri, Tofangchi and Afshar were his deputies. My time at Alborz College helped me to acquire the correct methods of reading, going through the extra curriculum and organising my thoughts and objectives. There was always a very tough competition amongst the students at Alborz, which meant that we were constantly aiming for high marks. The turning point of my life came when my parents decided to send me abroad for my university studies.

In those days, affluent Iranian families killed two birds with one stone and sent their children abroad for further education in some of the best universities around the world, as this would save them from being recruited for national service, should they fail to get a place in their desired course in Iranian universities.

In those days, my uncle, Dr. Karim Rokhnejad had returned to Iran from America after graduating from Columbia University. Daie

Karim, as we used to call him, had planned to emigrate to Australia for work and my father decided to send me to that country with him. He had heard that Australia was a land of opportunity with good weather and people, and had a progressive government, all the ingredients that would help his son to have a successful career. But how could I leave my home and family and go and live in a foreign land, without having their support and begin a new life all by myself? But apparently fate had decided that the river of life would take me away from my beloved country and I could not swim against that tide.

I wanted to become the eagle of Alborz and land at its summit but they were asking me to fly to a foreign land to open a new chapter in my young life. My future was destined to begin with leaving Iran and I could hardly oppose my father's decision, my entire life depended on his advice and directions and I had every confidence about his judgment, as a man who could see into the future.

My arrival in Australia opened the way for Nazee as she left Iran a few years later and first went to Switzerland and Canada for her higher education and eventually settled in California where our cousin Nasrin lived. Nazee did her postgraduate studies in psychology but both her and Nasrin now work in the finance and banking industries.

The news of my trip to Australia for university studies was given to the Shah. According to the courtiers' protocol, I went to his palace to say farewell and receive his consent. He told me that Iran and Australia did not have full diplomatic relations at that time and he wished me to become our country's first ambassador in Canberra after the end of my studies.

It was a dream job, which eased my many anxieties of leaving home for a foreign and distant land.

The Pahlavi Lands Trust paid part of my university fees and expenses between 1964 -1978 and this had led people in Australia to respect me very much as they thought I was the son of a member of the Royal Family. The international community always welcomed Iranians in those days and the country carried a diplomatic weight on the international arena. Whilst one could not compare the high standards of life in Australia with Iran then, there was every possibility that my country would achieve a similar position in the years to come.

We went to Australia via Indonesia but I was still not happy about having left my family behind. I had left a mother who had given me life, a father who had taught me how to live and a sister who was my best friend and confidante and who I had to leave so early in our teenage life. All these memories kept troubling me in my new life away from home. I could not connect to anyone too as the English language that I had learnt in Iran, during my studies at Alborz college, was different from the one that the Australians spoke.

I did not really know Australia well and had only a few mental images of the country before I arrived to live there. I had read things in books, like the kangaroos, the aborigines and the famous Sydney harbour opera house. Despite all their attractions, everything seemed unfamiliar to me. How could I replace Tehran and Iran with Sydney and Australia? I could never find a Manzariyeh in Australia where I could lie down on the grass and relax under the sun, or go to Mubarakabad and Abali on Fridays and spend the weekend at Royal Villa No. 9 where we would be amazed by its magnificent interior. How could I find new friends? - like the ones that I had in my Scouting group whom I would play with until nightfall!

Humans only appreciate the values of those assets in life once they have lost them. Just like a fish that has been thrown out of water and is bound to perish, I felt that I had been thrown out of my beloved country and was away from the source that sustained my life. I would remember my daily allegiance to the flag of Iran at the Scout camps' morning parades.

My mum told me: "It does not matter where in the world you are, as long as you remain an Iranian in your heart and soul. Without its culture, traditions, language and history, Iran is just one vast piece of land. You must always act as a good ambassador for Iran".

Her words of advice were a source of support and peace of mind for me in those days, even though I knew very well that despite what she told me, she herself could not tolerate being away from Iran and its mystic soil for even a day in her life. However, she was adamant that in my later years of life I would find out for myself what she really meant by saying that I must always remain an Iranian in my heart and soul and that I must be a good ambassador for the country wherever I went.

It was only many years after the revolution in Iran when I saw how impatient my parents were to return to the country that I understood the depth of the advice that my mother had given to me before.

My mother believed that my uncle Karim's experiences would always help me as he had already lived abroad for many years and had overcome the type of nostalgia that I had. But I could not possibly spend all my life with him. After all, he had a life of his own and his own family to look after.

He enrolled me at the Cranbrook School in Beverly Road. It was a posh and prestigious school in Western Australia, renowned for its harsh discipline. Its facilities were excellent and incomparable with the Alborz College. On my first day at the school I had this very strange feeling. No one was approaching me and the school's head teacher assigned two members of his staff to take me around the school and the city to get to know them better. I could not understand most of what they were telling me, and this confused me even further. I felt I just wanted to fly back to my own home at once.

I told my mother that something inside me was boiling and she told me that I had to give it time until it matured and gave me a new path in life.

Despite making several new friends, I still felt somewhat lonely. My first friend in the school was a young Jewish man and we spent many hours during the days together. At nights I either stayed with uncle Karim or chose to stay alone and say my prayers. Even though most of the members of my family worked at the royal courts, they were devout Muslims. I can safely say that my family had comfortably managed to reconcile their traditional values with modernity, the very preoccupation that had existed in the minds of our intellectuals and scholars ever since the Constitutional Revolution of 1905. The objective was to make sure that Iran and the Iranian mentality adapted to the modern world whilst we still remained a country with an old civilisation and culture.

Members of my family attended many posh and upper class parties, but never missed any of our religious ceremonies where they mingled with the common and hard working people. In those days, religion for our people was a means of finding a spiritual refuge in its moral values, before it turned into a way of seeking political and financial power.

No one had to pretend that he or she was a devout Muslim or was questioned about his or her religious beliefs; my family were loyal courtiers and faithful Muslims at the same time. We looked upon the caste of the clergy with respect. We all trusted them and regarded them as the custodians of our moral and spiritual values.

I clearly remember that the daughter of the grand ayatollah Kashani was our neighbour and lived next door to us. Every time the ayatollah visited his daughter, he would send their servant to collect my sister Nazee to go to their house and play with their children. Ayatollah Kashani liked my sister very much and he particularly liked the childish and funny questions she had for him. On one occasion she asked him why her father had to shave his beard every single day but the ayatollah had a long beard. We were told that ayatollah Kashani burst into laughter and had given his own humorous answer to keep the little girl happy.

The ayatollah knew my father very well and that he was a prominent courtier. Likewise, my family knew the ayatollah and they respected him and were on friendly terms with him and members of his family.

In those days I used to say my prayers on a mat that had been sanctified in a Muslim tradition, by taking it around the shrine of Imam Reza to get his spiritual blessing for whoever who prayed on the mat. Even though in my new life in western countries I gradually stopped praying in the Muslim tradition, I have never abandoned my faith and its human and spiritual values. If I used to go to my local mosque to say my prayers along with the other faithful, it was merely to take part in a tradition that reminded me of my moral obligations to do good deeds towards my fellow humans and the local community.

I would do a lot of charity works as well, and one of them was to feed the needy with sweet dates after they had finished saying their prayers in our local mosque. The local community was very pleased to see that the son of a courtier and a member of the royal family visiting the mosque and mingling with them. All the local traders and shop owners also knew me very well and they all tried to sell me the best sweet dates so that I could distribute them amongst the faithful in the mosque.

The first few weeks of my arrival in Australia passed with a great deal of nostalgia for back home and the difficulties of getting used to my new environment and life. But it was the advice of my parents that kept echoing in my ears that I must remain strong and hopeful as I embarked on a new path in life and I needed to remain steady and look forward. My mother's directions were particularly heartening, as, just like the Iranian mothers of today she wanted the best for her children and had no doubt that the hardships of life can only strengthen our determination to achieve our goals. I believe, despite the many restrictions that the present regime has put on the social, political and cultural life of Iranian women, that they are still a powerful force in the making of a new and democratic country.

During the few days that we stayed in Jakarta, our ambassador to Indonesia introduced us to an Iranian family. They were a very respectable Jewish Iranian family by the name of the Ghaderis. Mr. Jamshid Ghaderi was a well-known businessman and exporter of Persian carpets who had lived in Sydney since the time of Reza Shah. Even though the members of his family spoke in Farsi, his children who had been born in Australia were not that fluent in Persian language. It is only when one lives in an exiled life away from Iran that one realises how being able to speak in Farsi with your children is such a great pleasure; it is a great reassurance to know that you still have not forgotten your roots.

My father had written a letter to Mr. Ghaderi and asked him to do his best to make sure that now that I was away from Iran and living in a foreign land, I would still retain my Iranian culture and traditions. Mr. Ghaderi really did fulfil his promise to my father in that respect. He found a house for my uncle Karim next to his own residence which was an advantage for me as I could stay in touch with Mr. Ghaderi's family too every time I visited my uncle.

Time was passing very quickly for me, I still don't know why the passage of time seems to be faster outside Iran and I am sure every Iranian, who has lived abroad, would agree on this with me. By now I had several close friends I shared a lot of my time with, they helped me to settle in gradually and feel less nostalgic or alone. I had begun to look forward to my future instead of always wishing to go back to my old days. In other words, I had now entered into a period of self-realisation, confidence building and acquiring a new culture, which until only a few months before I had been reluctant to accept.

Then, there came a very defining moment in my life, when I met a Jewish girl. Why will my destiny always link me with the Jewish people? I still don't have an answer for it. Maybe because there were so many of them living in Sydney whilst only a few Muslims were there. But come to think of it, many Christians also lived in the city. First it was Mr. Ghaderi, the man whose kind help and assistance to me, during my first weeks of arrival in Australia, I will never forget.

Then, my best friend in Cranbrook School and there was also a Polish girl whose elder sister had perished in Auschwitz and was the only surviving member of her family. Was it our common feeling of being away from our homelands that attracted us to each other, or, her beauty and humility?

Her name was Betty Penny and she lived in the Bondi Beach area of

Sydney. Betty was my first ever love and I had become very dependent on her too. It did not really matter to me that she was actually one year older than me, even though then the age difference between a man and his future wife was an important issue for our family. It may still be the case, but does it really matter?

I had met Betty at a few parties and concluded that I had found the woman and love of my life. My young naivety and love for her led me to hide the fact that I was a Muslim from Betty and her family and they believed me too, as in those days, the Jews were a sizable part of Iran's population.

The more time I spent with Betty the more I loved her and could not see a life for myself without her. I could no longer hide my religion and told her the truth. As she was in love with me too, my religion did not matter to her at all and therefore she kept it a secret to herself and did not tell her parents about it. But fate had other plans for me.

An American friend of Betty's family was going to visit Iran and out of my goodwill I gave him the address of my cousins Saeed and Amir so that he could meet up with them whilst in Tehran. My cousins welcomed him to their family and entertained him during his stay in Iran but he betrayed us in return. When he met with the rest of my family, he noticed that we were Muslims and immediately wrote a letter to Betty's father and told him about this. After receiving the letter, Betty's parents became furious and banned me from seeing their daughter forever. My separation from Betty was a major psychological blow for me as she was the first ever love of my life and one can imagine what it meant to a young man away from his home and family, as well. It took me a great deal of effort to overcome my sadness for losing her, but time heals and gradually I went back to my normal student life, determined to rebuild it by aiming for high grades in my education.

As a private student I had to pay for my education and the fees were quite high, but my father looked at it as a way of investing in my future and happily paid them. However, the increasing cost of my education was a burden on my parents and my father suggested that he should sell one of his properties to pay for my fees but I rejected this idea and on the advice of my uncle Karim left my private college for a state run high school. In his opinion, which I respected, in a state high school I would benefit from mixing with young people from the lower and middle class. As it happened, I stayed in a state high school in Sydney and at the end of my course I left Australia and went to Canada for my higher education.

The main reason for me to go to Australia was to continue with my education without any interruption after my high school studies but many people could not do this in Iran, as we had to pass an exam to enter a university. Furthermore, the Australian government had entered the Vietnam War in support of the United States and as a citizen of that country I had to enlist in the Australian army. Returning to Iran was out of the question and I had to look for an English speaking country that did not have conscription either and Canada was the perfect choice for me. Together with uncle Karim, I emigrated to Canada, with my father still my main sources of support.

As I had already spent several years away from Iran and my family when I lived in Sydney, starting a new life in Canada was not that difficult for me, especially as by now, I was fluent in English and had grown up too. The only problem was getting used to Canada's harsh winter weather. The cold here went deep down into the bones but for someone who had overcome the demon of nostalgia for leaving Iran, getting used to sub-zero temperatures was not an issue.

We settled in Vancouver in British Columbia and I entered the Sir Winston Churchill School for the final year of my high school education before entering university.

I stayed in Canada until the end of my postgraduate studies during which time I met many of my future close friends who were to influence my career significantly. By now I had been away from Iran for more than five years and even though I had already met my mother and sister Niloufar in Australia, I still wanted to see the rest of my family back home. Niloufar had only been six months old when I left Iran and naturally did not know her elder brother at all. However, our blood ties soon made us very close to each other and the days that I spent with her and my mother in Australia were some of the most memorable times of my life. In a way, they represented the rest of my family by visiting me.

Sadly, during their visit, a poisonous insect stung my mother and its painful effects remained with her for many months after she went back to Iran. But I was sure that the joy of our reunion far exceeded her suffering and as the Iranian proverb says, mothers are willing to walk barefoot on rough land filled with spikes for miles if they know that their child expects them at the end of the journey.

By now I had accomplished the many objectives of my education and there was no doubt that I owed them all to the forward-looking advice and support of my parents. There are very many other Iranians like me around the world who have achieved similar high qualifications in the field of their studies. But sadly, most of them have chosen not to return to our country to offer their wealth of expertise and knowledge to their compatriots simply because Iran is currently ruled by a group of people whose interests lie in advocating ignorance and backwardness.

On my return from my visit to Iran, I enrolled at the University of British Columbia (UBC) to study the History of Fine Arts. On the advice of my father and in view of the then close relationship between Iran and United States, I decided to continue with my studies at the United States International University in San Diego, California. I did my doctorate degree in Human Behaviour & Leadership at the USIU and was looking forward to going back to Iran to serve my people and spend the rest of my life with my family in a country that I loved so much. Sadly, the destiny of Iran and her people was about to take a dramatic turn in a revolution that ended my dreams and those of millions of fellow Iranians. Not only could I not go back to Iran, my family also had to flee for exile like many other Iranian families, because the revolution had brought into power a regime whose mission was, and still is, to divide our nation between those who support its destructive policies and those who do not.

My father however remained optimistic. He still believed in the Shah and his loyalty to him would not allow him to see the reality that our country was on a slippery slope towards chaos and as it happened the revolutionaries would not settle for anything less than the Shah's downfall. I was in California when the Shah finally left Iran.

My father was hoping that just as had happened in 1953, the Shah would return to Iran and reassert his authority. My father could not possibly imagine that one day there would be a revolution in Iran and that the Monarchy would be overthrown. He kept saying that the Iranian people loved the Shah and would not leave him, but his over optimistic views proved wrong.

After the Shah's departure, my father left Iran and joined me in California. By now, Dr. Shapour Bakhtiar had taken over as the Prime Minister of Iran but his cabinet did not last long and collapsed when the army backed off and sided with the new regime.

Despite all the chaos and the wave of executions of army generals and former officials, my father still wanted to go back to Iran.

We warned him about his decision but he always said that he had done nothing wrong in life to deserve any punishment by the new regime.

However, as many of his close friends and associates were arrested and executed without trial and the country was going through the anarchy of the post-revolutionary period, we managed to convince him to postpone his return. He was however extremely worried about the safety of many members of our family as well as his friends and colleagues.

My father had one brother, Mehdi, and four sisters by the names of Banu Talaat, Banu Eshrat, Banu Shukat and, Banu Effat who had died at an early age.

My mother's family was however much larger. She had three brothers (Karim, Hussein who had died at a young age and Ali who has died recently) and six sisters (Banu Mehri, Banu Badri, Banu Fakhri, Banu Farideh and Banu Farzaneh). They all currently live and work in various countries of the world with their spouses and children.

Love for Iran never let my parents have a moment's respite and they were so impatient to go back and join the members of our family and friends. However, we kept postponing their trip by reminding them of the mass executions, arrests of former officials and the anarchy that the country was experiencing and, by now, the war with Iraq had also started which made their trip even more dangerous. They regarded Iran like if it was a parent and just like little children, they cried and begged to be able to reunite with it.

Despite all our efforts to stop them from returning to Iran, we eventually gave in to their demands and hoped for the best. Before their departure we thoroughly checked all their travel documents to make sure that they would not face any problems on their arrival, given the chaotic situation in the country.

We were so worried and anxious; both because our parents were leaving us and also the fact that we did not know what awaited them on their return. When we heard the news of their safe arrival, we breathed a sigh of relief. My father had first gone to the home of his mother to make sure that they were safe.

Everyone who had heard about the return of my parents rushed to see them as they had offered them nothing but help and friendship throughout their lives.

However, a group of opportunists from the village of Mubarakabad had filed a complaint against my father in his absence, claiming that my father had "plundered their wealth and oppressed them in the past" and that he had now returned from abroad to confiscate their land and savings and make them homeless. The simple-minded villagers had themselves confiscated our land in my father's absence and issued bogus title deeds for them, and by making this complaint, they tried to pre-empt any attempt by my family to recover our legally purchased properties in Mubarakabad.

My father behaved rationally and asked the Courts to decide on the case, and when the judge ruled in his favour, the villagers who, with their families, had benefited from my father's help and assistance over many years, apologised to him for their shameful actions.

Even though the court could not find any illegal ownership of land by my father in the course of the case, the new government itself had already confiscated some of the properties and changed their title deeds and refused to give them back to my family. This was now a routine practice against the former officials of the Shah's era, many of whom had left the country in fear of persecution. The new regime then distributed the confiscated lands amongst its supporters without the consent of their rightful owners, just to buy their loyalty and support for itself.

My father visited us on a number of occasions, but on his last trip he was unwell and the doctors diagnosed him with Parkinson's disease. The once strong-willed and active man who was my role model and, who in my childhood imaginations ruled the world, was now trembling with pain and could hardly do any work. Still worse was to come when he was also diagnosed with cancer. Later his kidneys stopped functioning properly and Alzheimer was added to his worsening health conditions.

Finally in 1992 the story of my father's life ended and he was laid in peace in a cemetery in San Diego, hoping that one day we would be able to return his remains to the soil of the land that he came from and loved and its people, up until the last breath of his life.

He left this mortal world with the peace of mind that his children had benefited from his valuable advice and had achieved a stable life in his absence. He left this world by leaving a good name behind as all those who knew Abbas Behbudi will testify to his honesty, loyalty in friendship, always seeking to help others in need and never involved in any wrong doing in his capacity as a courtier and the manager of the Pahlavi Lands and Properties Trust.

With my father's death, came my mother's anxieties and bereavement.

She could not cope with the loss of her life long partner and even her children could not compensate for this in any way. She could no longer live in exile without my father and wanted to spend the rest of her life under the sky of Iran, where she could find solace by staying with the rest of our family and the memories of her shared life with my late father. She still lives in Tehran.

I was in Canada when my father died. At the time I was living in Canada with my family as a Canadian citizen. I met my wife during a business trip to Greece. She was Susan Williams, a young woman who used to work for a major firm of architects, David Hicks, as a designer of large palaces. She was an expert in her field of civil engineering and despite her young age of 24 at the time, because of her enthusiasm and innovative approach, she was an assistant to David Hicks.

At the time, I was 31-years-old when I travelled to Saudi Arabia, on the invitation of Walid and Khalid Al Juffali, my Arab friends. The Al Juffali family were very rich and involved in the fields of electricity supplies and telecommunications and represented several major international companies in Saudi Arabia.

The Saudi environment did not attract me and in comparison with the then Iran, in terms of climate, social-economic progress and almost everything else, it was behind Iran and therefore after only three months I decided to leave the country.

However, during my stay there I travelled to Mecca and Medina and managed to find time for spiritual elevation by worshiping in their religious sites. I prayed for my family, friends and my country and wished them all peace and prosperity. During the Haj procession I had a very strange feeling that just by donning a simple white robe and staying away from the trappings of the material world, you could get closer to your Creator in the purest possible way, very much like the moment when one is born into this world. No wonder the Haj pilgrimage is the trip of a lifetime for anyone who wants to explore his or her true self and have a fresh start to their life and dedicate the rest of it to charitable and humanitarian works.

On my return to San Diego I began to work for an oil company by the name of Destiny Petroleum on the advice of my friend Robert. The company was involved in oil and gold explorations, and during my employment with them I earned a sizable amount of capital through my work and investments. Eventually, I decided to buy some of the shares of a gold exploration company in their mine in Arizona.

As a young and energetic businessman I was working very hard round the clock and travelled regularly across the US, Europe and Asia. By now I had invested in many other business projects, including building a shopping centre and investing in the oil and gold industries. In Texas and in search of exploring oil fields I rented a vast land in partnership with one of my Canadian friends. After discovering oil in the area we drilled a number of oil wells in it for further explorations and this was the beginning of my entry into the oil market in earnest.

According to American Law and regulations, the underground natural reserves of any land anywhere in America belong to the owners of the property once they are discovered and explored. In a short period of time this land and its black gold changed my and my friend's lives forever.

By now we had entered into the oil market and were involved in doing business with the major international companies. Gradually we began to buy the shares of other oil companies too and one of the most important of them was Oxon Oil.

Just before my fortieth birthday, on the advice of one of my friends, I decided to build a restaurant in one of the beach towns of Greece. It was both fun and business and we thought we could kill two birds with one stone by having a relaxing holiday in Greece at the same time as we oversaw the progress of our building project.

However, the trip lasted six months and it was during this time that I met Susie. A very motivated and attractive girl, she quickly changed my mood from a hard working businessman into a romantic lover. Once again I could hear the throbs of a heart that was searching to find the love of his life to share this world with, under a shelter as wide as the blue skies of the world.

After many years of loneliness, love had once again entered my life. I looked at myself in the mirror. I was now a 40-year-old man who had conquered the many summits of his ambition in life and had huge wealth. Many people knew me around the world but I still had to re-discover myself in a different capacity and so when Susie organised a memorable 40<sup>th</sup> birthday party for me, I used the occasion to propose to her. I had found the love of my life and without her I was like a bird unable to fly.

We left Greece together and went to England to get engaged in the presence of her parents. I had to leave London for California immediately after our engagement party, Susie joined me months later and we married in 1989. Now Susan Williams had become Mrs Susan Behbudi and I was so pleased and happy about it. We had a wonderful honeymoon and as for most of our engagement period we had been apart from each other, the honeymoon trip was a great opportunity for us to plan our shared life ahead. We decided to have our first child who was a girl. In the old days, parents could not know the sex of their offspring during the mother's pregnancy but new medical technology had changed all that and we now had the opportunity of preparing ourselves in advance.

However, there was still some anticipation and joy in waiting to be surprised by the sex of one's child when it arrives in this world.

I congratulated my father on the birth of my daughter as he had now become a grandfather, but I could sense in his voice that he was hiding his true feelings from me. I thought maybe he would have loved me to have a son first but soon found out that he was as happy about the birth of my daughter as the rest of the family. Every time she cried or smiled she made us feel like we were all a part of a happy family. My father naturally wanted to see that his family would continue through his grandchildren and carry his name. As far as I was concerned, I had now reached the highest stage of my life achievements by becoming a happy father and husband, a feeling that one can only express verbally but never be able to describe its spiritual dimensions.

I could see my mother's face in the features of my daughter. We named her after my mother's name Forough, but chose the English name Elizabeth for her too so it will be easy for Susie and her family to call her. After all, she was Susie's daughter too, and we now had our own little "Queen Elizabeth" in our home!

Our second child ended some of the family's jibes and completed our family as it was a boy and in the Iranian tradition we now had an "accomplished family". Overnight all my father's concerns about the continuation of his clan's name disappeared and he was now over the moon with happiness.

Although the arrival of my son was a great blessing on the family, sadly my father could hardly even touch or hold him due to his failing health and the devastating effects of his Alzheimer disease. But he kept saying with his usual philosophical and deeply spiritual approach to life, that my son had come to this world to pave the way for his departure from it, as such is the rule of existence.

He would say this in a way as if he knew his death was fast approaching, and he would not be around to see his grandchild stand up and walk.

We named our son Abbas Noah, in memory of my father and in respect for the followers of all the religions of the world.

Today my son Abbas does not remember anything about his grandfather, as he was only six months old when he died. He departed from this mortal world to find his place in the hereafter.

After his death and in deep bereavement, I lost my motivation for work and a social life for a period. My life had become a quiet and sad one. This was a particularly difficult time for me as my mother had returned to Iran to live the rest of her own life with the memories of my deceased dad.

However, I came out of my depression by fulfilling my promise to my father that I would always look at the bright side of life, work hard, protect my family and never allow the ups and downs of life to halt me.

I began to concentrate on my work and my wife and children provided me with their support and gradually helped me to come out of my bereavement.

My constant involvement with the oil industries and markets, as well as my international investments and trips had turned me into a successful and well-known businessman. Although I was an Iranian-American, I did not have much contact with Iranian communities and did not know them well enough, as I should have, for a man who loved the country of his birth.

I began a comprehensive study of my fellow Iranians inside and outside the country, with an emphasis on the course of the social, political and cultural changes that had taken place amongst them over the previous few years. I certainly used to follow the news about Iran before then but I decided to analyse the news one step deeper below the surface.

In 1997, Iranians and the world community were shocked by the news of a massive earthquake in the Province of Khorasan where several thousand people died. Unable to deal with this colossal natural disaster, Iran had asked for international help.

I was devastated by the news and asked myself how best I could help. I finally decided to act on my own and immediately contacted the Iranian embassy in Ottawa.

I spoke with the then Iranian ambassador Dr. Adeli and asked him to let me have a list of the emergency items of aid for the people who had suffered in the earthquake. He sent me a 15 page long list of the medical and logistic items that were needed by the Iranian government to help the affected people.

Just by coincidence, at the time I was researching a number of sources about Islam, Christianity and Judaism, in the context of the history of Iran and various religions of the world. My intention was to discuss my research findings and points of view with certain religious leaders of the world at the time in a forum so that we could create a better understanding amongst the followers of their religions for a peaceful and better world.

In my view, all the religions of the world emanate from one spiritual source and have only taken a different form as a reflection of their time and the impact that their propagators have made on them when presenting them to their followers.

There is only one God for all of humanity, no matter if we are Muslims, Christians or Jews, and we are all accountable to Him for our actions. He will always treat all his children with justice and will never discriminate between them.

The differences and clashes that are advocated amongst the various religions of the world are only the work of bigots and hypocrites, for whom religion is a business and a tool in promoting their own self-interest and power.

Even worse, in this day and age, we have certain "religious leaders" who claim to represent God on Earth, when they do not even believe in God in Heaven.

All I am trying to say here is that the criminals, who kill their fellow human beings in the name of God, have nothing to do with the essential message of Religion, as no true believer in God could ever harm his or her fellow beings, let alone murder them in the name of religion.

We believe that the killing of a human being equals the killing of humanity as a whole and that is the magnitude of perpetrating a crime in the name of religion.

I am a Muslim and come from a devout Muslim family but I will never, ever condone any disrespect for any other religion in the world and their followers. In fact, I have always chosen most of my best friends from amongst the followers of the various religions in the world as we always share the common principles of humanity between us, as in the case of my efforts to help the victims of the earthquake in Iran,

I contacted a group of my Christian friends who were involved in international charitable activities. I asked the Rev. Pat Robertson, who has a TV program, to help us organise the task of sending aid to Iran.

Some of my friends were concerned about the lack of security in Iran for those traveling to the country and that was most deplorable for an ancient country renowned for its tradition of hospitality throughout its long history. As the founder of the Charter of Human Rights, we now had to worry that the lives of foreigners visiting our country in order to help us was in danger from their hosts!

What else but the acts of the present rulers of this country can be blamed for this unfortunate disgrace? One should shed tears for this injustice done to Iran and the Iranian people.

I accepted all the responsibilities for this aid project and reminded my Christian friends that Jesus is the Prophet of Love and that, therefore, they should not miss this opportunity to follow him and offer their love and support to the victims of the earthquake. I told them that very much like themselves, I disagreed with the current rulers of Iran, regarding their actions as inhumane, and very much believed that they have no respect for humanity and the rights of the people of Iran.

They only tolerate people who agree with their policies even if they are criminals. However, what is at stake now is the desperate needs of the Iranian people and not the interests of the ruling regime, and we must respond to that.

I finally managed to convince them and a week later they put together a consignment of all the supplies that were needed for the earthquake victims.

I contacted the Iranian embassy and spoke with Dr. Adeli. I told him that there were a number of conditions that his government had to fulfil before we would send the aid to Iran. First, they had to renew my Iranian passport. Secondly, two of my American friends would be traveling with me to Iran and the embassy must issue a travel visa to them and, thirdly, the Islamic Republic must undertake the responsibility of safe passage of the consignment through Iran, and pay for the delivery of the goods. He quite happily agreed to all of my terms and provided us with the necessary help.

However, the lack of trust was not only from our side, as he also

assigned one of his staff to inspect the contents of the consignment
to make sure that it did not contain any illegal items. They officially
confirmed that the goods and logistics were of the highest quality
possible, and this proved that we had no intention other than to help
the victims of the earthquake.

After many years of living abroad, I was now returning to Iran again.
On the plane they seated us in the VIP section in appreciation of what
we were doing, and in particular to show to my American friends
a taste of Iranian hospitality. Of course this was during the time of
Mohammad Khatami's presidency; I read to myself a poem:

*"the joy of reunion with one's love is like a cloud raining upon a*
*thirsty man in the desert"*.

True, I was like a thirsty man who had been away from Iran for
many years. I just wanted to run around, yell and breathe in Iran again.
I was lost for words in describing my feelings of being back in Iran
again. It was as if I had been reborn. It all seemed like a dream and I
was not sure if it was happening to me in the real world.

I had come to my fatherland and it had opened its arms to me, to
its son who had learnt from an early age to love it. At the airport,
I kneeled and kissed the soil. What did the people around me think
about what I was doing at that moment, and what was going on inside
of me?

They did not know that even if you own the world and have the
most comfortable life, you are still homeless if you do not live in the
country of your birth.

People looked at us in a kind way and appreciated what my friends
and I had done. My family, relatives and friends were equally kind
to us and there were many moments when we hugged and cried with
tears of joy.

Together, with my American friends, we went to Khorasan province.
I took them to visit the shrine of Imam Reza where they were amazed
by the magnificent architecture of the site and its mosques and were
constantly filming. What they did not know was that this splendid

artistic and cultural heritage was not confined to Mashad only. It was also to be found in Isfahan, Shiraz, Yazd, Kashan and, indeed, all over Iran.

We went to the areas devastated by the quake. Nature had savagely destroyed the lives of many thousands of families by killing their loved ones. In some cases whole families had been buried alive under the rubble.

People were numb and could no longer even weep over their misery and the remains of what had once been their home, where they had lived with their children and wives, now it had all been lost and swept away. What was Nature trying to achieve when it had so savagely ended the lives of so many innocent and weak humans by shaking the Earth?

The province had been declared a disaster zone and the survivors' lives were in immediate danger. Everyone was doing his or her best to help. Despite the many man made miseries that had befallen the nation over the last few years, the deep sense of humanity that Iranians have, at times of national crisis, was still in evidence and at work in there.

At that time, the Ettelaat Daily reported that an Iranian who lived in Canada had donated 1.5 million dollars to the aid of the victims of the Khorasan earthquake and had personally travelled to the country to share the grief of the victims over their loss.

Later, the Payvand Weekly in Vancouver also published an article on this humanitarian action and praised all those behind it.

My American friends returned to the US after a few days but I wanted to stay and see many other people and places, and enjoy my trip to the fullest. Borrowing a quote from the famous Iranian poet Forough Farrokhzad:

*'my eyes were hungry to see as much of Iran as I could possibly look at'*.

Tehran had changed enormously. New highways, modern apartments, roads, cars and shops were everywhere. The young population looked very smart and prosperous and followed the latest Western fashions and styles.

University students had advanced both in terms of academic ambitions and their socio-political rights. They were very conscious of the important role that they were playing in building a new country and demanded freedom and democracy for the nation as a whole. They aspired to achieve and enjoy the political freedoms and human rights that Khatami had promised them and the nation when they had voted him into office. For a long time their dreams of a democratic country had been suppressed, and in Khatami they saw a glimmer of hope. They were like birds in a cage, waiting to be released so that they could spread their wings and fly.

When Khatami wept in public at the time of announcing his candidacy for the second term, he was indirectly telling people that certain powerful circles, behind the scenes, were plotting to dash the hopes of the nation and its youth for a better future, and intended to bring their full dictatorial policies back to Iranian politics.

Contrary to my concerns, during my stay in Iran I was never harassed or interrogated by any government official or security agent.

Even when I went to the registry office to change my birth certificate, nobody questioned why I was still holding a birth certificate that had an Imperial stamp of the Shah's era on it, but just changed it for me. Again, on my way back to Canada I came across no problems at all.

On my return to Canada and having been impressed by the hopes and vigour of Iran's young population to build a new and democratic country, I decided to help the Iranian people in any way that I possibly could. This led me to think for hours and hours how I could best achieve this goal. I was not a politically minded individual, at that time, and with the help of a group of Iranians, we decided to find a way of building new fraternal bridges between the Iranian and American people.

We were also thinking about how best we could help with the health problems of the rural poor in Iran and for this we approached many American specialist physicians and doctors, for advice and help on this humanitarian issue. We were aiming to make it easier for the Iranian and American scientific communities to contact each other and exchange their knowledge between them. In short, we just wanted to do something positive for the sake of the people of the two countries, as doing nothing would amount to submitting to defeat and that did not agree with my character.

However, after many months of hard work, we arrived at a stalemate and concluded that the problems of my fellow Iranians and the country were far greater than the capabilities of a group of experts and could only be solved when the nation embraced democracy. No matter how dedicated we were in helping our fellow Iranians from abroad, as long as tyrants ruled the country, every effort in this respect would be in vain.

I then decided to help Iran's youth in achieving freedom and democracy by writing articles in the major American newspapers. In these articles I tried to show the real Iran and why the international community must distinguish between the desires of the Iranian people and the dictatorial regime that rules over them.

I argued that our people belong to a country with a long history of advocating peace and justice for mankind through their culture and art.

I was particularly determined to introduce the true faces of Iran and the Iranian people to the American people. At the same time I wanted the Iranian people to learn more about the views of American and Western thinkers on the merits of democracy and freedom to help them in their own struggle for these noble ideas.

However, as I did not have much knowledge or experience in this type of political activity, I decided to start my project with some modest planning. I asked Mr. Bahraloo, a veteran radio and television journalist and Ms Nazanin Afshinjam, a prominent human rights activist, to work with me on the project. We also approached the Reuters News Agency for the purpose of renting one of their studios, and we launched our own satellite television of World International

News WIN-TV.

In the beginning, we had a daily one and a half hour program for our US and Canadian audiences. We were planning to expand our broadcasting time and reach a wider audience inside Iran itself, but sadly differences of opinions amongst the staff halted our expansion plans. I decided to employ an American manager for the station to run the channel, but after a while, we once again ended up in that condition of confusion and stalemate that so often characterises everything Iranian.

The closure of the television channel was met with mixed responses from the public. Some began to criticise me volubly with unfounded accusations and others expressed their regret and chastised me for dashing their hopes. The latter's criticism, however, was still very encouraging in that it reminded me that I must not withdraw from this fight.

WIN-TV was a subsidiary of the Council for a Democratic Iran (CDI), which I had established three years previously. The main objectives of the CDI, in addition to those that I have already mentioned here, is to create an association of respected, trusted and professional Iranian individuals and groups to work together with the aim of achieving a lasting democracy and human rights for Iran.

The Council's activities are currently going as planned.

I constantly meet educated and professional Iranians, who share my dream of our Motherland being free from the tyrants who currently rule it, and who wish to help the Iranian people establish a lasting democratic system of government in the country.

Certainly, bringing together the wealth of expertise, professionalism and dedication of so many patriots into one body will be very beneficial to the cause of democracy and human rights in Iran. I have already made it clear that each individual or group that joins our Council is entitled to hold onto their political or religious beliefs, as long as the liberation and progress of Iran towards a truly democratic and civil society remains our joint objectives.

Political arguments and ideological difference can always be debated through mutual respect for one another's opinion, but what is now at stake and demands our joint urgent action is to liberate Iran from the claws of the present tyrannical regime, and bring peace, prosperity, human rights and progress for our beloved country - Iran.

In this holy mission I welcome everybody, whether young and old, religious or non-religious, Muslim or non-Muslim, man or woman who believes that Iran must be free and belongs to all Iranians!

# Ideas and Vision

*As expressed through interviews with the press
in six chapters*

## CHAPTER 1

### *Interview with the Kayhan of London Weekly*

# Introduction to the Council for a Democratic Iran (CDI) and its Objectives

*"We must prepare ourselves for the establishment of a democratic system in Iran."* - Behrooz Behbudi

## Background:

Dr. Behrooz Behbudi is a well-known figure amongst Iranian communities.

He has been tirelessly involved in the fields of community and charity work for many years and has recently begun his political activities, specifically with the objective of establishing and promoting democracy in Iran, so far he has made significant progress in this respect. Iranian communities now regard him as a successful and influential politician.

Dr. Behrooz Behbudi is the grandson of Suleiman Behbudi who was a loyal and trusted private secretary to the late Reza Shah of Iran. He began his early studies in Australia and continued them at Canadian and American universities and after achieving his doctorate, successfully entered into industrial activities and business.

Dr. Behbudi is one of those successful Iranian businessmen who has generously used his financial means for the service of his home country in order to help his fellow Iranians.

After the earthquakes in Khorasan and Bam, he rushed to the help of his countrymen and women by donating millions of dollars to their aid. In 1998 he set up the Council of the Global Unity Partnership with the help of one of his American friends, whose mission is to arrange dialogue and build a bridge of mutual understanding between the different cultures and religions of the world.

In 2009, Dr. Behbudi established the Council for a Democratic Iran as well as the satellite television channel, WIN-TV, in Washington.

Unfortunately, due to some internal problems, WIN-TV stopped broadcasting about a year ago. The main objective of the Council remains the establishment of a democratic Iran. Dr, Behbudi's articles are regularly published in Kayhan of London, as well as on the Council's website. The readers of Kayhan of London are familiar with Dr. Behbudi's points of view on many social and political issues.

However, we have now had an interview with Dr. Behbudi, where he provided further information on the Council's aims and activities.

* * *

**Dr. Behbudi, you have been a successful businessman and have, in recent years, entered the world of politics too. Our readers know you to some extent through your articles in Kayhan of London. We also know that you are the director of the Council for a Democratic Iran. But before we come to the question of the Council's activities and aims, you have become a successful businessman through your hard work and higher education in US and Canada and you are a rich man. Usually, those Iranians who are involved in business activities avoid entering the world of politics and some of them do not even trouble themselves to think about the problems of Iran and its people. What has motivated you to enter politics and Iranian affairs?**

_ Thank you for your time. I must say that I am also surprised to see that many Iranians who live in Western countries and have sufficient financial means do not pay much attention to the problems of Iran and the Iranian people. As for myself, I come from a family that has been involved in the political affairs of Iran, and its members have held political power, in one way or another, over many years.

Besides, there are many thousands of people like me who in the not too distant past used the resources of our country and studied in the advanced countries with the hope of returning to Iran and serving it. Obviously, with the circumstances prevailing in Iran, many of us could not possibly return after our studies had finished and had to stay in foreign countries. But I do not believe that this change of circumstance, should change our aims or responsibilities and, therefore, we must try to utilise our expertise and the means at our disposal to help and serve our country and its people.

I have always felt indebted towards Iran and our people because I believe we cannot part with our past. It was Iran and its people who made it possible for us to travel abroad and study in the major universities of the world and later on, to become successful businessmen and women.

If we did not have these national resources in the first place, we would never have achieved what we have now. Therefore, we must always try to return the debt that we owe to our country and its people.

**Before we talk about the aims of the Council, there is a question that in all your articles and speeches you insist on the need for achieving democracy in Iran more than anything else and that democracy is the main priority for you.**
**So much so that it appears that even in the event of the overthrow of the Islamic Republic regime and a change of government for Iran you believe that the objective of achieving democracy must still continue. Can you explain this please?**

_ You are right. I believe that democracy is the answer to all of Iran's problems.

I went to Australia for my early education, when I was very young and later went to America and Canada to continue with my higher educational studies. I have lived in many advanced countries of the world for long enough to make me think and research about the reasons for the progress that Western countries have made and why our own country has not been able to do the same, even a hundred years after our Constitutional Revolution.

Some may think that democracy and its rewards are only compatible with Christian societies, or that the natural and human resources that these advanced countries have, is the reason for their success. I have concluded that none of these factors is the reason for this gap between the advanced and the backward countries.

I'll give you the example of the two Koreas, North and South Korea, or the former East and West Germany. They are all the same people, living next to each other and with almost identical social, economic and environmental characteristics.

But when it comes to prosperity, security, freedom and progress we see two different nations; one which enjoys freedom and democracy for its people and is an advanced country and the other is engulfed in backwardness, repression and insecurity and is at odds with the Free World.

After years of studying the root causes of these differences I have concluded that democracy marks the absolute difference between an advanced or backward country. All the advanced and progressive countries of the world have democratic systems of government; regardless of the type of regime they have, whether a monarchy or a republic. What really matters is the democratic nature and content of the system, not the form.

As for our own country, we must bear in mind that in view of the current developments in the region, the religious dictatorship that rules Iran will eventually collapse and be overthrown. But if the Khamenei-Ahmadinejad regime is replaced with yet another type of prettified dictatorship then nothing will have changed and our problems will stay and get even worse.

That is why I believe that the only way forward for Iran and the Iranian people is to start moving on the solid foundations and tracks of democracy on the same day that this regime is overthrown.

**You established the Council for a Democratic Iran in 2009 after your experience of the Council of the Global Unity Partnership. Can you tell us more about the Council's objectives?**

_ As I explained before, I believe that what Iran and the Iranian people really need is the establishment of a democratic system of government. We cannot achieve this goal, by way of slogans and issuing statements or talking about the merits of democracy. The struggle for democracy starts right now, before the life of the current dictatorship ends. We must begin to create the foundations of democracy. That is why I established and launched the Council for a Democratic Iran, which embodies a group of our compatriots from amongst experts, academics, politicians and human and civil rights activists. The Council has offices in Washington, New York, Paris and Vancouver.

**What practical steps and activities has the Council had so far in line with its objectives?**

_ We believe we must prepare the ground amongst our fellow countrymen now if we want to achieve a democratic Iran at a later stage. Those Iranians who live in the Western and democratic countries of the world already enjoy the democratic freedoms that democracy has provided for them and they understand the mechanism of a democratic government or system.

The members of the Council have done extensive research and studies on how to implement these democratic values and principles in a future Iran. Undoubtedly there must be a distinct separation of the executive, legislative and judicial powers in order to guarantee a truly democratic system. On the other hand, a democratic system is founded on the creation and functioning of political parties, associations, civil institutes, trade unions, and most importantly of all, a free press and media.

People must have a say on the formation of government bodies through the power of the vote and the State must guarantee the public's freedom of speech and that of the Press so that they can express their desires and, at the same time, control the authorities to make sure that they will not act against the Law and the Articles of the Constitution.

We must do the necessary research in this respect and prepare the appropriate civil programs to implement them. The Council has been continuously involved in these types of educational and practical activities and we have drawn up specific plans and programs for issues ranging from traffic problems and the creation of manufacturing units to arts, culture and education.

**It appears that in order to achieve these aims the Council may need to rely on the help of other organisations that may not necessarily be part of it, such as other political parties and opposition groups.**

_ In fact, one of our programs is to invite other Iranian political parties and groups to cooperate with us in achieving our united aims.

We take for granted that other Iranian opposition groups also aspire to democracy for Iran, except a few organisations whose main objective is to get power and then set up their own type of dictatorship and we will have nothing to do with them. All political groups and organisations can be a member of the Council and at the same time keep their independence and identity whilst cooperating with each other in order to achieve our joint objectives.

**You have established the Council for a Democratic Iran. Can you describe your own definition of Democracy and what it entails in your view?**

_ The history of Democracy goes back to ancient times. According to the Iranian historian, Bastani Parizi, in ancient Greece people had to vote for everything, including when they could get drinking water. Though this may sound a bit exaggerated, we must not forget one point and that is that despite the long history of democracy amongst civilised nations, the political philosophy of democracy is not that old. I mean the democracy that we are currently referring to is a contemporary and modern phenomenon.

Although the term democracy is universal, everyone has a different interpretation of it and it is very difficult to have one single definition for it, as this depends on various conditions and factors, like culture, history and the history of the country in which democracy rules.

Naturally, the way that a European trade union activist will interpret democracy is different from the experience of a poor farmer or labourer in an African country. This does not mean that the African worker is less human, but it just goes to show that there are many differences between the countries of the world, in which we live,

We do not have to call it an African nation. Let's just assume that we are talking about an imaginary country whose people are denied education, housing, health and prosperity and people are constantly fighting to feed themselves and their families on a daily basis, just to survive.

Certainly the people of this imaginary country will hardly have the luxury of having the time to think about anything else, let alone democracy.

The word democracy as we know has a Greek root and means the rule (crates) of the people (demos), or, more precisely, the power of the people and their sovereignty over themselves.

If we accept this principle of democracy, which is the rule of the people over their own destiny, then we must look at the factors and the instruments that can bring about democracy and turn it from an idea into reality.

The right to rule over one's own destiny is the essence of democracy. It is directly related to the ascent of mankind to a higher status of social well-being as the people's knowledge, about the social conditions of the country in which they live, is crucial in this regard.

Nothing will ever happen as long as the people do not aspire towards Democracy or they are purposefully left ignorant of its benefits. Let's not forget that all tyrannical regimes resort to any means available, including torture and repression by the Armed Forces in order to keep their hold on to power.

Therefore, public awareness and a desire for a progressive improvement in the quality of life is always in confrontation with despotic rulers who are armed to the teeth in order to stop them achieving their democratic goals. The path to democracy in undemocratic societies is a long and difficult one.

Sometimes, some regimes will themselves initiate this process towards democracy by coming up with misleading slogans and plans but, in due course, their deception always gets exposed. The communist regimes of the last century and the current regime of Iran are good examples of these fake democracies.

In a democratic society, citizens cannot all take part in the day to day running of the government's affairs as this will lead to anarchy, hence the idea of choosing their representatives in order to oversee this process on their behalf.

Perhaps it can be said that the true and democratically elected representatives of the people, in the organs of the government, are the best definition of democracy.

The advantage of this democratic ideal is that if a representative fails to deliver in his duties to his constituents then they can remove him or her from their position and replace them with someone who is more suitable for this job.

What really matters in selecting these representatives is how well qualified they are to carry out their duties, regardless of their religion, colour or social background, we can see that in the United States a coloured man born into a Muslim family can become the President.

In a democratic society, people are a collection of independent individuals who live in harmony alongside each other, with everyone being able to think and judge for themselves about the conditions in which they all live under, as opposed to being a mass of people with no individual identities.

Achieving this individualism is another symbol of modernism and, therefore, democracy is linked to humanism, where the human element, its desires and needs become a principle of democracy.

When we believe that in a human society, all its individual members have equal rights and are free then we arrive at the conclusion that humans, freedom and equality are the foundations of a democratic society and without any one of them, the notion of a democracy will become meaningless.

In a democratic society, there is no Big Brother watching you, nor is there any hierarchical order amongst the citizens, as they are equal to one another and have equal rights. The main mission of the State in this democratic society is to strive towards delivering the highest levels of prosperity and security to its citizens, whilst, at the same time, protecting its rights.

### Is this not a Marxist or Socialist definition of democracy?

_ They may be similar in their definition of democracy. But unfortunately the Communist countries picked up a good idea and after advocating democracy, once they had rallied the people behind their slogans, they walked towards establishing tyrannical regimes of their own.

One of the fundamental aspects of a democratic Society is to create the conditions for its citizens to think freely.

In democracies, governments do not obstruct the freedom of thought and do not regard freethinking and creative ideas as being in contradiction with their rule. This attitude or system of government never happened in the former Soviet Union. If you study the history of the Stalinist era, you will note that a great many thinkers, scientists and artists were either jailed by his regime or had to leave their country and go into exile. Many writers had to use pseudonyms to get their articles or works published without being persecuted by the state. It is true that the Soviet leaders talked about creating a classless society, but in reality and, in practice, this classless society was just for the majority of the people under their rule, as they themselves had created their own upper class, which was above the rest of the population.

In a democratic society, nobody can imprison dissidents. They always listen to what have to say and cannot take the law into their own hands. The state must be at the forefront of upholding the law not abusing it.

The late Ali Akbar Dehkhoda, the renowned Iranian scholar once said in his satirical paper, Charando Parand, that in dictatorial regimes, the MPs in their rubber stamp parliaments believed that they were one step above the law and that they could trash it as they wished. This tyrannical view of the law and its function does not have a place in democratic societies as the law is the very foundation on which Society stands and citizens live by.

The same people who are in power in Iran used to shout many nice and attractive slogans in praise of democracy and freedom when they were opposing the previous regime. But in reality none have been achieved.

One needs to ask these people if you opposed the previous regime, for as you claim, it jailed and tortured its opponents, then why are you doing the same with your own dissidents? What is the difference between you and the previous regime? What was that revolution for? - if after so much bloodshed and destruction we are back to square one and none of the slogans of freedom and independence have come true?

**But in the Iran of today, all the aspects of a democratic system of government such as a parliament, a president and so on, do exist.**

_ Yes, you are right. But how effective and democratic are they? Did we not have parliamentary elections in the pre-revolutionary era?

The present regime in Iran does indeed hold many elections in the country but they have a vetting system in place, which disqualifies those whom the regime regards as "unsuitable".

In other words, the regime dictates to the Iranian people that they should only vote for those whom the regime selects, in advance of the elections.

**But the regime says that if it does not do this vetting system then anyone could come forward and claim to represent the people!**

_ We did talk before, about the issue of the public's awareness and its high level of education and understanding of its rights in a democratic society. We either live in a democratic society or don't. There is nothing in-between. If the rulers of Iran claim that they have established a democratic country in which the people are conscious of their rights and civil liberties, then it must not insult their intelligence by telling them that 'you people don't know your rights and I must decide for you'. You can't have it both ways.

Besides, in a democratic system the armed forces of the country have no role to play during elections or side with the winners against the dissident, opposition groups.

The post-election events of 2009 prove that the ruling regime in Iran is not a democratic system and does not even respect its own constitution. Is it not in the Constitution of the Islamic Republic of Iran that citizens have the right to organise rallies and take part in demonstrations so long as they do not insult Islam? Then why did the regime react in such a brutal way against those peaceful protestors who were just asking about what had happened to their votes for the opposition candidates?

This is a fundamental and civilised question to be asked in any democracy that claims to have a mandate from the majority of its citizens.

As I said before, in a democracy, people are always in a position of asking questions and holding their leaders to account and the leaders' constant job is to convince the public and serve them.

In his 'historic' speech after the outburst of protests against the result of the elections, the leader of the Islamic Republic called the action of the protestors as 'waging a war on the State by bringing an army of people onto the streets'. He then said that people must end their protests and just go home and obey his orders. He needs to be asked, if bringing an army onto the streets, is an act of war then why did he do the same by deploying the armed forces onto the streets against the Iranian people and allowing the country to fall into the deep crisis and misery that we are witnessing today?

**In your opinion, is there any direct correlation between democracy and the economy?**

_ Democracy in the spheres of economics is the same as free markets. This means that the same freedom that people enjoy in electing their representatives in their preferred system of government, must equally be applied to the economy so that people can choose the type of goods or services that they require for their everyday life. In democratic systems, governments are no more than the coordinators, not arbiters, of this electoral process and the provision of freedom of choice for their populations.

This means that in a democratic system, various social groups interact amongst themselves on the basis of the law and the regulations of society, free from the interference of the State. As these social groups do not depend on one another for their economic survival, they treat each other with democratic norms and mutual recognition, whilst the government acts as a coordinator between them.

In contrast to dictatorial regimes, in democratic societies, it is the government that depends on these social groups not vice versa, and there is always a dialogue between those groups and the government in order to make sure that the peace and progress of society is maintained.

The government does not have the right and cannot, actually, interfere in the rights or affairs of these social groups as it will lose its own rights and interests as these groups pay a proportion of their profits to the State in the form of taxation in order to make sure that the State protects their entities.

This process leads to the creation of wealth and capital, which, in turn, increases production and creates competition in a free market.

In dictatorial and undemocratic systems, this process is reversed. Here all social groups owe their economic existence to the central government's intervention, as the State is the largest business entity and has the exclusive right to the production of one or several sources of revenue for the nation.

The capital and the wealth that is earned through the export of these exclusive commodities are all paid into the accounts of the government and the State distributes it amongst the citizens and as it never relies on receiving taxes from the citizens, it never enters into any mutually beneficial economic, or social-political, dialogue with the people. This lack of an organic link between the State and the people will eventually lead to a major rift between them, where each have their own agenda and outlook on society.

In the former model of society, the capitalists who operate and produce their goods and services, free of the State's intervention, within a market economy, accumulate wealth and capital but have to make national contributions by paying tax to the government, which uses it for public services.

But in the latter system, as the State does not consider itself being dependent on receiving taxes, it never establishes any proper taxation system for the overall population and runs public services from its own pocket. Therefore, tax evasion is the norm in those societies.

**To this end, democracy and capitalism work hand in hand. Then do you not think that in this system the public are the losers?**

_ Not really, the less the State interferes with the affairs of enterprises and their free market activities, the more it finds funds and opportunities to serve the public. After all, in democratic countries, governments are elected by the pubic in the first place to serve their interests first.

We must not forget the fact that capitalism no longer exists in the world in its original entity and this may be partly due to the effects of Marxist and Socialist ideologies.

For example, in countries whose economy is based on capitalism the State pays a huge amount of money for public services such as national health insurance. In the case of the National Health Service in Britain, health services are offered free of charge to the public through the taxes that the government receives from the entire population, whether you are a civil servant or a rich capitalist.

The distribution of these taxes through the provision of public services does away with inflation in the economic system of the country as, at the end of the day, it is based on the notion of spending the people's money on themselves without the State having to contribute to it from its own sources of revenue.

**They seem to have taken some steps in Iran to implement a similar capitalist system by legalising the privatisation of industries.**

_As you rightly said, some steps have been taken in Iran to establish a kind of capitalist system but, here again, very much like the supposedly republican system of the regime, many contradictions exist.

The regime has huffed and puffed about removing economic barriers so as to allow the privatisation process to succeed but just like many other claims made by it, this issue has to be accurately studied in order to establish the truth.

The regime keeps publicising the privatisation of certain industries and banks even though the proper foundations for these reforms have not been laid down, and we end up with a further re-nationalisation of the industries and banks by the State.

I do not mean State-run capitalism, but Crony Capitalism in which the regime's leaders appoint their cronies to run these industries by making them rich through access to huge public funds whilst cheating the nation at the same time.

When the Iranian government constantly interferes in the micro and macro affairs of the country's economy, the result is that all those companies and enterprises that take part in government tenders and win them are actually the State's own subcontractors.

When the Revolutionary Guards Corps is the most powerful enterprise in Iran and runs most of the industrial and construction projects of the country, how can you expect to have a free market capitalist system there?

Earlier, I mentioned that there is a direct correlation between democracy and capitalism. When despots rule in a country then to expect that privatisation and capitalism will flourish is simply a waste of time. In such a society, the public are the main losers, as they have to endure hard economic conditions, inflation and economic corruption, in addition, to having to live under the repression of a tyrannical regime.

Naturally, at one point, all these pressures will give way to a burst of public dissent that will cause the system to collapse. Ignoring these pressures and economic crises will pave the way for the emergence of fundamentalism and political violence.

**But we already have this fundamentalism and political violence ruling in Iran, do we not?**

_ Yes indeed, you are right. Maybe I should have said even more fundamentalism and social strife. Given the dogmatism and religious bigotry of the present regime in Iran, there is absolutely no chance that this regime will ever distance itself from its ideological radicalism.

This is a regime whose fundamentalism has only brought about insecurity, crisis, strife, poverty and misery for the nation of Iran.

However, we must not forget two points about the term fundamentalism.

Fundamentalism within the context of humans striving to promote fundamental values of life is not, in itself, a bad thing. What makes fundamentalism abhorrent is when it seeks to gain political power through radicalism and violence and acts as a reactionary force against progress and modernity.

The other point is that, in my opinion, there is no direct relationship between religion and the current understanding of fundamentalism. In fact, whilst religious fundamentalists claim that they are reverting to the fundamentals of their religion, their wrong and misleading interpretation of the message of their religion is damaging the image of their faith and turning people away from it, as is happening right now in Iran.

### What are the characteristics of this type of fundamentalism?

_ To start with, they fanatically believe that whatever they say and think is the absolute truth. Secondly, they all have a fundamental problem with modernity and its aspects. A glance at the plight of the intellectuals in Iran proves these points.

Recently the regime's 'academics' have embarked on removing Human Sciences from the education system of Iran, as they claim that these subjects are Western oriented and can corrupt the minds of Iranian students and thinkers.

Nothing can be further from the truth. They are in fact afraid of the power of Human Sciences to defeat their own weak and shaky ideology in philosophical arguments. Human Sciences advocate the methodology of asking questions with a critical approach amongst academics and students, whereas these gentlemen are only interested in people following their despotic regime and blind orders like a flock of deaf and dumb sheep.

If Human Sciences are 'harmful', then why did thousands of clerics, before the Revolution, study them in our universities in order to acquire the latest education and knowledge and then present themselves as intellectuals to the nation? The point is that the same clerics were then thirsty for power but now that they are the ones in power, they have deceitfully forgotten their own past.

The main feature of this type of religious fundamentalism is its authoritarian and dictatorial approach to social and political matters. It has absolutely no flexibility or tolerance and employs violence and brutality to attain its objectives.

It dons the cover of religion and is not prepared to listen to anyone, to the point of insanity. The Iranian people have been paying a heavy price as a result of the rule of these fundamentalists who are seemingly at war with the entire world.

At the time of Hashemi Rafsanjani's presidency, his administration was planning to turn Iran's state run economy into a free market economy, similar to the models that exist in Turkey, Malaysia, Brazil and Argentina.

However, Khamenei opposed the idea and now after 30 years we can see where those countries stand and what an economic mess Iran has become.

CHAPTER 2

# Iran's recent history – A Review

**Some people think that the Iranian people are not mature enough to achieve democracy and then argue that the presence of the people in the Friday prayers or government-run religious gatherings proves this. What is your opinion on this issue?**

_ You need to ask those who have this assumption 'who are these people that attend the Friday prayers and what percentage of the Iranian nation do they represent'?

Attending religious gatherings and ceremonies is different from going to Friday prayers. Whilst Friday prayers are a religious gathering, the way the present regime organises them, they follow different objectives, we can safely say that the office of the leadership determines beforehand what Friday prayers imams must say during their sermons to the point of putting words into their mouths, thus making them ridiculously similar wherever they may be delivered in the country, in other words, these are political shows, not religious gatherings.

Most of the people who attend them are the supporters of the regime. Tehran has a population of around 13 million people. The number of people who attend these Friday prayers in the capital does not even reach one million. At the same time, the religious gatherings and ceremonies like the mourning of Imam Hussein in Ashura are completely different in their nature. Despite the regime's attempts to turn them into political events by sending its own paid mullahs to attend them, the people never take part in these ceremonies as a sign of their support for the regime. These are spontaneous ceremonies that reflect the religious sentiments of the Iranian people.

We cannot deny the fact that Iranian society has its own traditional and religious values, which were behind the victory of the Revolution but which have been abused by this regime in order to stay in power.

**You mentioned the Revolution and how the clerical regime has abused the religious sentiments of the nation. Can you expand on this please?**

_ The clergy in Iran began a process of self-assessment in the 1930s and stepped outside the traditional boundaries of the theological schools and seminaries by studying the works of Western philosophers and political thinkers. The books that have been written since then by some theologians in this respect are sufficient proof of this new trend. They are books criticising Marxist theories, books on Realism and so on, which indicate that the clergy had begun a process of in-depth study of modern and contemporary philosophy in order to be able to enter polemical arguments with them. But now and in a break from their tradition they also entered Iranian universities both in their capacity as lecturers in Islamic theology, as well as students and researchers.

They no longer regarded the learning of languages other than Arabic as 'apostasy'. Ayatollah Beheshti, who lived for many years in Germany, could speak several major languages of the world.

In line with this new approach, they still kept sending their missionaries to the remote rural areas of Iran, where in contrast with the modern cities the population still remained very religious and traditional.

However, there was a problem here too, as, for the clergy to run its missionary works; they had to have their own source of finance. Some of this came from the religious taxation and contributions that were being made to the houses of the grand ayatollahs that oversaw the work of these missionaries. However, they still needed more financial support and that is where the Iranian bazaar merchants entered the scene as one of the traditional allies of the clergy in Iran. Their network of financial channels, not to mention their wealth, meant that they became one of the most powerful supporters of the religious establishment during the Revolution of 1979.

The clergy's political and economic ambitions gradually turned into powerful opposition against the Shah's rule, with the mullahs now claiming that the monarchical regime posed a threat to Islam.

The religious forces also took advantage of the work of dissident intellectuals like Al Ahmad and Ali Shariati and advocated a return to Islamic values in order to save the religion of the country from the excesses of the Shah's rule.

Whilst the missionaries were busy mobilising the peasantry in the villages, the Islamic intellectuals were publicising their ideas amongst the urban and middle classes.

It is true that at one time the Iranian people were led to believe that their religious values and beliefs were in danger from foreigners, as more and more Western culture was being imported into the country. However, the clergy only took advantage of this concern in order to promote their own reactionary doctrine of Islamic government, which was later to become the tyrannical regime that now rules the population and decides on every private aspect of the life of its citizens whilst taking the country back to the Dark Ages.

Regrettably, this regime has a religious façade but its deeds are detrimental to the religious beliefs of our people. Nowadays for Iranian people, the true religious traditions and ceremonies are only those that they used to attend before this regime came to power because this regime has turned every such occasion into a political rally in support of its policies and justification for all the abuses that it carries out against the Iranian people.

**What is your preferred model of government?**
_ I believe that Iran must be ruled by a secular democratic system.

**But in view of the religious beliefs of the Iranian people, do you think they will welcome a secular system of government? If such a system were to be established in Iran, what are the chances of it surviving in the long run?**

_ In my view, wherever in the world, religiously based institutions have come to power; they have corrupted the system to its roots. The history of the world is packed with examples of those regimes that have abused religion as a means of remaining in power and achieving their own objectives and, in turn, making people hate their own religion.

Just have a look at the history of Christianity in Europe. How committed are the European people to their religious beliefs today? The main reason for this, in my opinion and in the view of many, is due to the Reformation of the Church and its representatives in their relationship with the people and their aspirations.

The Church had become the absolute ruler and could not possibly forego the many luxuries of wealth and political power that it had amassed by sucking the blood of the people and by abusing religion. Any force that threatened, such as scientific discoveries, the Church's privileged position, had to be suppressed or destroyed completely. The case of Galileo versus the Church is the most crystal example of this.

But at one point the people rose up against their medieval and tyrannical rulers and in the process destroyed whatever the Church had built over many centuries. In this battle Christianity was the actual loser, a religion whose principles were in complete contrast to what the clergy and the Church had been doing in its name for their own interests.

In my opinion, even if Iranian people do not begin to hate their religion and their traditional religious beliefs, then, at the very least, they have begun to question the legitimacy of a regime that rules over them in the name of their religion. It is this lack of legitimacy on the part of the regime that is challenging its very foundations now and certainly threatens its existence too. No wonder that the regime of the Islamic Republic constantly suppresses any channel of debate on the history of religious government in the world by portraying itself as the representative of God on Earth.

In this so-called Islamic government, the absolute ruler claims to occupy the same position that the prophet of Islam once did and thorough this links himself to God. This is exactly the same position that the Church and the Christian clergy once claimed to represent.

However, we have here an ideological tug of war between the young generation of Iran and the followers of the Islamic government of the absolute leaders, or Valiye Faghih.

I have no doubt that one day this tug will break and that the followers of the Valiye Faghih will be thrown out of the scene and this will be the unavoidable verdict of history.

Those who come to power thereafter will stop the experience of the Revolution from being repeated again.

**Does this mean that a secular regime will come to power?**

_ Yes indeed, but a secular regime is not after the negation of religion. It only advocates the separation of the State from Religion and that religious beliefs must not interfere with the running of Society. Religious beliefs are a private matter for every individual and a secular government has no business in interfering with them. As a matter of fact, with a secular government in power people will enjoy more freedom to exercise their religious rights. However, this means that under such a secular regime, the clergy must be confined to their mosques. This is essential and out of respect for the religious traditions themselves.

In the Iran of today, the clergy claims that they are protecting the religion of the people, but in reality they have divided the nation between those who support them and those who oppose them. Their position is that if you are not with us, then you are against us. This reactionary stance has led them to purge many of the educated and academic elite from the country's institutions. As a result many thousands of our educated people have left Iran to work in foreign countries or live in exile.

This reactionary view towards educated people has forced many of our senior academics to resign or to seek early retirement.

In fact, as well as plundering the natural and economic resources of our country, this regime is also involved in destroying Iran's human and intellectual capital. The regime's purges are not only confined to those who do not subscribe to its reactionary ideology but also include the very people who helped it to come to power in the first place. Many of them are now either in prison or under house arrest.

In my view, the main problem here stems from the fact that despite their influence on the Iranian people, the Shia clergy had never been able to form a government of its own in the country and now that they have, they are not prepared to leave this position that easily.

If you study the history of Iran carefully, you will note that the Shia clergy only held to some local power in the northern provinces of Iran while the rest of the country came under the influence of the Sunnis.

We have a long history of the Shias being massacred by the Sunnis in the past, the most notable incident occurred in the city of Ray, which was conquered by the Sunnis at the cost of killing thousands of Shias.

There may have been a time in our history that the Shias enjoyed majority rule in Iran, but those periods were always very short lived.

However, in the history of Iran after the arrival of Islam, the clergy never ruled the country as a political force, even during the time of the Safavid dynasty when Shia Islam became Iran's official religion. Therefore, by all accounts, this is the first time in our long history that the clergy has established a national government in Iran and it is not surprising that they are now fighting with tooth and nail to protect and sustain it.

In the process of establishing this socio-political power for themselves the clergy have effectively transformed many of the traditional religious institutions to keep their hold on power.

The regime regards itself as the sole custodian of Islam and it believes that if it falls then the religion of Islam will disappear too! This hypocritical justification is the very basis of every type of tyranny, religious or not, which lead to the horrific crimes that have been committed by this regime.

Dictatorships always fear pluralism. They are blind and deaf to other opinions and voices and all they can hear is the echoes of their own propaganda. You can see these evil characteristics in every aspect of this regime. Everyone is expected to serve one dictator and follow his orders.

This mentality has poisoned the relationship between the regime and the people and weakened the people's religious beliefs as whatever crimes the regime commits, they subscribe it to Islam and their faith.

This is exactly what happened in Europe under the rule of the Church.

In a future democratic Iran, people will only be judged for their contributions to Society within the framework of the Law, irrespective of their individual religious or non-religious beliefs. The truth is a wholesome subjectivity and is not confined to any single ideology or religious belief.

## So you believe in pluralism?

_ Precisely. In my opinion pluralism is the hardest enemy of authoritarianism.

Principally, pluralism is intertwined with democracy. When you do not hear any voice other than the propaganda of the regime in Iran then this indicates that the ruling regime is not democratic. To stifle the voices of dissent, the regime resorts to crackdowns, jail, torture and the execution of all those who dare to raise their voice.

Pluralism is based on respect for the rights of others and accepting the fact that truth is not the property of any single individual. If we accept these principles then there is no place in our society for questioning other people's beliefs. It is only under tyrannical regimes that one despotic ruler claims to be the holder of truth and the rest of the people have to obey him as a flock of sheep who needs his direction.

**Will this then allow the government to spend its time on sorting out the greater issues of the nation such as their progress and prosperity?**

_ Absolutely. Just look at the amount of time and energy and budget that the regime spends every single day on various methods of interfering in the most private matters of its citizens. The armed and militia forces are constantly engaged in telling the nation what to wear or not to wear or how women must do their make up! In no advanced and civilised country of the world would you come across this nonsense.

In every country of the world, there are certain laws or code of conduct for citizens to follow in order to avoid social strife and ills. For example, it was in the news that the British government was considering a ban on the import of certain clothes for young people that could incite them to commit sexual violence. Banning this item with the support of the public is different from raiding people's homes to find out what t-shirts or make up they wear.

The regime in Iran considers itself as the guardian of the Iranian people and a judge on whether they should go to Heaven or Hell.

It gives itself the right to order them on what they should do and how they should think every single day of their lives, or arrests and jails them whenever it wishes to do so, without it being held accountable for its actions to anyone in the world.

**It appears that the authoritarian and intrusive nature of the Iranian regime is not only towards the citizens of Iran as the regime also tries to meddle with the affairs of other countries as well.**

_ That is true. For decades now, this regime has been doing its best to fan the flames of war in Lebanon, Palestine and Israel by supplying arms to those extremists who share its insane policies that supposedly seek to annihilate the Jewish state. It wastes billions of dollars of the nation's money on destructive plans, instead of spending it on the burning needs of the Iranian people.

The regime pays a great deal in bribes to Latin American countries, such as Venezuela, to continue their supposedly anti-American polices. They spent huge amount of money on arming their puppet groups in Afghanistan and Iraq to destabilise those countries, just to prove that the Americans are bogged down in them. They have spent so much and caused so many casualties, all for the sake of nothing.

In fact, the Islamic Republic regime has all along wasted the wealth of the Iranian people on issues that have, in turn, only created enemies for the nation ever since it came to power.

**Iran justifies this by claiming that the money is spent on the Palestinian and Lebanese groups as part of its regional defence policies to pre-empt a military threat against itself.**

_ To prevent what military attack? From whom? Why should we create an unnecessary enemy for ourselves in the first place and then spend billions of dollars on defending ourselves against it?

I cannot understand the logic behind this mentality.

When a country so openly declares war on another and says it must be wiped from the surface of the Earth, just what do they expect to receive in return? The world is not a battlefield and countries must respect certain international and accepted norms and conventions and this is not limited to the State of Israel alone.

Immediately after the Revolution, some elements of the regime seized the American embassy in Tehran and held its staff hostage for more than a year. At that time a certain faction within the regime supported this disgraceful action and called it 'the revolutionary occupation of the nest of spies', disregarding the fact that an embassy of any country is part of the land of that country in a host nation.

If there were any problems between Iran and the United States why could they not have solved it through civilised and diplomatic channels? We have had far worse problems with the former Soviet Union in our past history but managed to solve them. They occupied the northern half of our country at one stage and annexed several of our provinces to their own country. Right now they are plundering our oil and gas in the Caspian Sea. Should they do anything more to deserve to be called 'an enemy of the interests of our country'? But the regime regards the Russians as a friend. Why didn't they seize the Russian embassy?

In my opinion the anti-Americanism of the regime is simply based on its hypocrisy and only the Iranian people have to pay a heavy price for this insane policy. The regime has invented its own norms and criteria for political and diplomatic relations with the rest of the world that have, in practice, paralysed the lives of the Iranian people. Take the example of the international sanctions against Iran.

The rulers of the country claim that sanctions have had absolutely no effect on the economy of the country and they actually welcome them. But the suffering Iranians will tell you a different story on how they have to bear shortages, rations, inflation, poverty, unemployment etc. that the sanctions have brought about.

**What do you mean by the regime's 'invented diplomatic norms'?**

_ For example an individual in the leadership of this regime publicly announces that the State of Israel must be wiped off the surface of the world. Later this miscalculated comment, which is against all accepted norms in international relations between the countries of the world and the interests of the Iranian people, becomes the official foreign policy of the country. All this because at one stage in the past Khomeini had said the same thing.

Here, one individual makes an insane comment and puts millions of people at the risk of a conflict in Iran, as well as in Israel and Palestine. It affects the lives of millions of Jews and Muslims alike.

If you talk to the Palestinian people, many of them strongly believe that the Iranian regime's interference in the Arab-Israeli conflict is the main reason for the continuation of hostilities between the two nations.

In a secular and democratic Iran, one individual cannot decide on behalf of a nation and invent his own laws and doctrines on what foreign policy the country must have.

## Why must Iranian-Israeli relations be like this?

_ Iran has been meddling in the Arab-Israeli peace efforts for many years by not recognising the right of Israel to exist as a country and at the same time by providing military and financial support to those extremist groups who seek the destruction of the Jewish State. The Iranian regime has never answered a basic question as to why is it more Catholic than the Pope on this issue as many Palestinians support co-existence with the State of Israel.

For many years now the wealth of the Iranian people has been spent on this insane policy in the name of sympathising with the suffering Palestinian people. If the regime is honest in its claim, then why does it not offer the same sympathy to the Syrian people? Instead of which it supports the Assad regime that kills them. Humans are all the same regardless of their nationality, there must be no difference between the Palestinians and the Syrians when it comes to supporting human rights and values.

It is quite obvious that the regime's support for some Palestinian and Lebanese groups has nothing to do with human rights and is just a cover to justify its hateful foreign policy, which is based on this destructive interference in the affair of other countries.

When the regime keeps calling for the annihilation of the State of Israel then no one can be surprised that the Israelis regard the rulers of Iran as their enemies.

If the Iranian regime's excuse for this policy towards Israel is based on its opposition to the repression of the Palestinians at the hands of the Israelis, then how could they justify the savage repression of their own people during the post-election events of two years ago?

The regime defends its crackdown on the protests against the results of the election by saying that they threatened its existence. It means that the regime had a 'right' to defend itself. If we accept this excuse, then why does it not give the same right to the Israelis to defend themselves against those who threaten its existence? Is it not then a fact that this regime has occupied Iran and represses them like a foreign and occupying army?

**Is your preferred secular regime a monarchy or a republic?**

_ I have already made this point clear in many of my previous interviews that what really matters in a system of government is not its form but its content.

Monarchy or Republic are just various forms of a system of government. They are nothing more than names.

There are many monarchical regimes in the world that are democratic, like those in Britain, Austria, Sweden, Holland and even in Japan in Asia, whilst we have some so-called republics that are, in fact, amongst the most tyrannical regimes of the world. The Islamic Republic of Iran, the North Korean regime and the Syrian Republic are the worst examples.

We must bear in mind that in all these monarchical regimes, the Kings or Queens are only a symbol of national unity and their post is ceremonial and they are paid by their governments to carry out this job.

They have no power to interfere in the affairs of the country and are constitutionally barred from entering politics.

But in Iran today we have a Supreme Leader whose powers are above those of the State and he has the right to interfere in every business of the government and the affair of the citizens.

He appoints ministers for a president who has been elected by the people. Parliament has no independence from his meddling and MPs cannot oppose his decisions and must act as his subordinates.

He has set up a body called the Guardian Council to monitor Majles bills and legislation to make sure that they conform to his personal opinions. He is the real foreign minister of the country and every official must follow his orders on Iran's diplomatic relations with the rest of the world. If he says that 'America cannot do a damned thing', then nobody must say anything about how this insane policy has ruined the country.

If we study the contents of the Supreme Leader's speeches, we can notice how most of his verbs are imperatives. How could one individual possibly be able to determine what is right or wrong for a nation and at the end not even be held accountable for what he has said or done? It is no surprise that faced with this question; his cronies have raised the position of the Supreme Leader to being equal to that of God's! When Almighty God is the ultimate source of knowledge and is aware of what we think and do, then the Supreme Leader as his representative on Earth must, therefore, have the same power.

With the type of unlimited power and immunity that the present regime in Iran has given to its Supreme Leader, it makes it a completely new and unique phenomenon in the history of political systems in the world, which, in fact, sounds more like a joke than a reality of our times.

This regime is an amalgam of many contradictory elements. It calls itself a republic but is actually headed by an individual whose power far exceeds the monarch that it replaced. It is involved in destroying the faith and culture of our people in a manner that no other foreign invader has ever done in our long history.

In the past, if a king did anything that was considered to be wrong and against the interests of the people his misdeeds would not be blamed on our religion. But nowadays, the Iranian people are turning against their own faith and condemning it for the actions of a regime that claims to represent Islam. It is an undeniable fact the many of our people, especially our young generation, have no faith in Islam and hold the faith responsible for the dictatorship that rules the country.

During the time of the Shah, some of our grand ayatollahs never advocated an Islamic government as they could foresee the disastrous consequences of such a reactionary step.

**The points and opinions that you have expressed here are more or less the same demands of the Green Movement in Iran. How does your model of democracy and government differ from the one proposed by this movement?**

_ The important point that we need to note about this movement is that the levels of its demands have changed since its inception.

Today you cannot claim that the followers of this movement still demand the same objectives that Mir Hussein Mousavi was asking for when the movement was born.

In my opinion the main problem with this movement, at the time of its inception, was that it insisted on reforming the present regime, whereas you cannot reform this regime at all.

The leadership of this movement did not have any problem with the religious nature of the regime and only wanted to see some reforms carried out here and there, within the existing order. Some dissident elements in the regime still believe that democracy, secularism and political Islam can coexist alongside one another. This is where I and people who think like me about the future of Iran differ from them.

As you know, the majority of the Iranian people have now surpassed the leadership of the Green Movement in their demands and are calling for the overthrow of the religious regime in Iran. This position is principally in line with my objectives.

CHAPTER 3

# The future of Democracy for Iran

**We were discussing the Green Movement in our previous chapter. What do you think this movement represents?**

_ The Green Movement was not born overnight nor will it die overnight. That is why it is a deep rooted social movement that is currently the main challenger that the regime has faced to the extent that its very foundations were shaken. We can point at many causes that led to the emergence of this movement, causes that have taken shape over the period of many years but burst into open at the same time.

The main cause of this movement can be said to be a public dissatisfaction amongst the various social groups in Iran and their consensus about the root causes of the problems that they have had to face in their lives.

This type of social unrest usually starts at a low level and then gradually finds momentum when conditions become ripe and on this occasion the fever of the elections and the widespread rigging of the votes provided the right opportunity for the outpouring of the public's grievances against the regime.

The regime denied the public the opportunity to seek change through peaceful means and this added to the wrath of the people. However, even though the public could have easily used their potential to seek change through violence when they were on the streets in their millions, they still managed to control themselves. In contrast, the regime used the excuse of the presence of a few elements whom it called "misguided by the enemy" to launch its bloody crackdown on the people.

It could even be assumed that these certain elements were the regime's agent provocateurs who were trying to discredit the genuine movement of the people.

When the regime announced on national television that a young man killed in the disturbances has been its own spy whose cover had been blown by the enemy before being murdered, then how can we expect it to have the slightest decency and honesty in anything that it does?

While some may liken this movement to the events that eventually led to the 1979 Revolution, for a number of reasons I must say that this is not a similar uprising nor is the regime able to adopt a policy to silence it.

We can still vividly remember the regime's crackdown on the opposition forces in the aftermath of the Revolution. The country was at war, the economy of the country was not in the mess that it is in today, as the Shah's legacy of foreign reserves were intact whilst mass media and fast internet communications did not exist at that time. All these conditions worked in favour of the regime to crack down on dissidents by mass-executing them.

But we now live in a different world and conditions have changed significantly. That is why I believe comparing the Green Movement with the anti-regime currents of three decades ago is not rational; the outcome for the Green Movement will be something quite different.

The country's economy is in a desperate shape. Inflation has broken the back of millions of working families. In the midst of all this economic mess, the government has introduced its subsidy reform programme, which, at the end of the day, will lead to even more economic hardship for the population. All these factors will stop the government from being able to repress the movement systematically.

**But the regime did crackdown on the Green Movement and has**

**even killed many of the movement's supporters.**

_ That is true, but you cannot draw a comparison between this crackdown with the previous ones. The mass media came to the help of our people and exposed the crimes of the regime to the international community. Worldwide condemnation of the regime increased and it became even more isolated because of its gross abuse of human rights. The regime has responded by saying that this is an internal issue and that foreign countries have no right to interfere in Iran's affairs, but all the indications are that the regime has retreated under international pressure and lowered the level of its crackdown.

They released a few prisoners and allowed some others to go on parole and even organised a kind of court hearing to look into the crimes that had been committed in the Kahrizak detention centre where the post-election protestors had been held.

Although all the regime's reactions did not result in any substantial benefit to the people, nevertheless, they showed that the regime had been acting from a position of weakness.

The regime chose to take the battle into a different field and, as with all its Machiavellian policies, tried to use the power of its media to discredit the opposition by accusing them of supposedly playing into the hands of foreign powers in the eyes of certain sections of Iranian society.

I have already talked about how Iranian society has still kept its traditional values and the way that the clerics actually abuse these values for their own earthly gains, in the same way that they did during the course of the Islamic Revolution.

In the case of the anti-regime protests on Ashura day, the regime accused the demonstrators of being agents of the Israelis and the foreigners who wanted to insult Imam Hussein. It then organised its own pro-regime demonstrations to condemn the opposition forces. A quick comparison between the number of people who attended this pro-regime rally with those who took part in the mass demonstrations in support of Mir Hussein Mousavi will give an indication of the weakness of the regime in the face of the opposition forces.

In line with his deceitful policies, the Supreme Leader openly cried during a meeting with his associates about the Ashura anti-regime protests and claimed that he had spoken with the missing Imam, a ridiculous attempt to justify his regime's hypocrisy.

The Iranian people are used to seeing him sob deceitfully to cover his abuse of power every time the regime comes under public scrutiny for its savagery against them.

I do not, therefore, deny the fact that the regime has resorted to many crimes against the Iranian people, but I will add that it has now lost its previous resolve to do so as it has become aware of the fact that the more it crackdowns on people then the more they become united to challenge it.

If the Green Movement protestors were only asking about what had happened to their votes, then the regime's harsh reaction forced them to heighten the level of their demands and reach a point that directly questioned the legitimacy of the Supreme Leader. Therefore, from the regime's point of view a temporary retreat was considered to be a better tactic as the movement would have become even more radicalised and many more people would have joined it.

One must also not forget that the Islamic Republic regime is very sensitive about losing its 'prestige' and it claimed that it in view of its 'Islamic principles and the interests of the country', it was prepared to forgive the opposition leaders and as has been the case since its inception, it began to offer its pardon to those who repented.

In my opinion, to this day, the regime still does not know what it should do with popular opposition movements. The crackdowns, massacres, prison sentences and organisation of pro-regime rallies and its portrayal of itself as a victim of foreign and internal plots have all failed to quell post-election turmoil and the movement that has been born out of it.

It is interesting to note that the supporters of the Green Movement use every opportunity to demonstrate their opposition to the regime.

One day they come out in support of the democracy movements in the Arab world, and the other day they mingle with the government organised rallies and shout their own slogans. All the indications are that this movement is alive and continues to go forward by reshaping itself.

**In view of Mir Hussein Mousavi and Mehdi Karobi being under house arrest, what future do you see for the Green Movement?**

_ It is true that the Green Movement began its life with Mousavi and Karoubi, but I believe that the movement's objectives changed half -way through and went beyond what these two leaders stood for. You could see this change of direction in the slogans that the people were shouting in the streets. Whilst Mousavi and Karoubi were still insisting on keeping and reforming this regime, the people's demands were more radical.

The statements by Mousavi and his calls for protest rallies and demonstrations acted as a platform for people to come forward and express their demands, but we must not forget the role that the Internet and the cyber channels played in this respect too.

Our young people use these channels to connect to each other and coordinate their protest actions and the regime is fully aware of the power of the Internet and has done its best to disrupt it in any way it can.

Despite putting Mousavi and Karoubi under house arrest and effectively imprisoning them, the flames of the movement have not been extinguished. The public has not yet been convinced and whilst the regime claims that the "conspiracy has been defeated", you can sense its never ending fear that the movement might re-emerge. The regime knows very well that the crackdowns have not produced a victory for it because it has not given the public what they had asked for.

I see this situation as a powder keg that is only waiting for a spark, when that happens, no power or crackdown will ever stop the people, especially if they get the backing of the army too.

Another point is that this movement is not dependent on any single individual and must not become the exclusive property of any political group inside or outside the country.

What really matters here is that all Iranians, wherever they may be, who long to have a democratic and progressive country must unite to achieve these aims irrespective of their personal preferences.

**You mentioned the role that the Iranian army could play in any future changes in Iran. Do you think the army is different from the Revolutionary Guards?**

_ Yes indeed. Iran's armed forces are generally divided into the national army and the Revolutionary Guards Corps, each of which have their own sub-divisions. The Basij militia force is a subordinate force under the command of the Guards and played a major role in the crackdowns on the people during the post-election protests.

Members of the Basij militia are selected from amongst the uneducated and the fanatics who are then brainwashed into blindly carrying out the orders of their commanders and violently attack and harass members of the public and dissidents with impunity. They are a Gestapo-like force who are kept in reserve by the regime to use against its opponents.

For example, in the case of the assassination attempt on the life of Saeed Hajarian, the architect of the reformist movement, the assassin was a well-known member of the Basij who avoided jail and was later actually given an official job by the regime.

Members of the Basij introduce themselves as the servants of the Supreme Leader and this title gives them a licence to kill or break the law as they simply lack any intelligence and have been brainwashed into behaving like zombies.

They are in the pay of Khamenei who controls them like robots. For many years now Khamenei has been donning a check scarf around his shoulders, which is worn by all members of the Basij militias, pretending that he, too, is one of them. The Basijis look up to him as their "God" and kiss his footprints to show their loyalty to his leadership.

You cannot expect a young fanatic, who does such a repulsive act of obedience to another human being, to be in the right frame of mind.

No wonder when the Supreme Leader orders the Basijis to crackdown on someone, they will go for the blood of that victim as they have been brainwashed into thinking that their crime will be rewarded by God as they have killed an enemy of the Divine. They expect to land in Heaven the moment they die.

However, the Iranian army has different characteristics. They are still the legacy of the former monarchy. They are educated and have a wide range of modern military skills. I cannot deny the fact that within the army there may be individuals whose loyalty lies with the religious regime, which is quite natural given the influence of their social background. However, unlike the Revolutionary Guards, the Iranian army regards itself as a nationalist force and is closer to the people than the Guards are.

After I wrote an article on this subject in the Persian weekly, Kayhan of London, I received many messages from inside Iran that indicated that the army has retained its overall independence and does not act as a mercenary force for the regime in the same way that the Revolutionary Guards and the Basijis do.

One young colonel wrote to me and said that this regime regards the Iranian army as its "step-son", implying that there is no real trust between the two and this is not surprising given the extent of discrimination that the regime directs against army personnel whilst it looks after the Revolutionary Guards.

The same army Colonel has told me that his salary is half the amount of what a Major in the Revolutionary Guards receives.

He also reveals that the members of the regular army who choose to live in military bases are constantly harassed by the security forces stationed on the bases. Members of their families are picked up for ignoring the full Islamic hejab cover and for returning to the bases after 9pm, when they have spent a night out with their families or in town. In short, the Iranian army is a potential enemy of the regime when it comes to choosing between the people and those who rule the country.

The regime indirectly acknowledged this fact by assigning only its security forces, the Basijis and the Guards to face the demonstrators during the post-elections riots and protests, as it feared that the army might join the people.

The same Colonel has told me that Iranian army personnel are aware of the regime's unpopularity and the fact that it acts against our national interests and that when the day of reckoning comes, they will side with the people to topple the regime. I believe one of the major tasks of the opposition forces in exile must be to unite the dissatisfied members of the army and even the Guards with the democratic movement.

**Talking of the opposition forces, how do you assess the power of the exiled dissident groups?**

_ There is a phenomenon called "round table discussions", in political terminology, it refers to an opportunity for a dialogue between people, whether they share many aims and objectives, or whether they have a clash of interests. The logic of "the round table" is that no particular party, which sits around it, is superior to the others. Everyone has an equal right and position vis – a – vis the others. It is only during the dialogues and civilized discussions between the attendees around this table that the righteousness and legitimacy of their arguments become apparent as our great poet Saadi puts it: "Not until a man speaks his mind shall we know about his flaws or arts".

It is only through these discussions that we can find out about our common objectives or our differences. Those who believe in overcoming their differences with their opponents through goodwill and tolerance will magnify their common aims, but those who think narrowly and lack goodwill, will insist on differences. This is a general rule.

We have all seen these round table discussions where leaders of different countries attend a meeting to talk about their common problems or objectives. The interesting thing about these round table talks is that despite the deep allegiance of the delegates to their own points of view, at the end of the discussions they will agree with the consensus of the meeting.

I had to mention this introduction first before talking about the so-called Iranian opposition forces in exile and their actions. Sadly, 30 years after the Revolution in Iran and despite all the political, economic and cultural opportunities that the dissidents have had to organise a meaningful fight against the Islamic Republic regime, to date, their efforts have not produced any tangible results or made any inroads.

We have not had one single round table summit amongst the members of the opposition groups and individuals up to this day. They have always sat around a long and rectangular table, indicative of the divisions amongst the attendees. At times, the agenda of their meeting has been overshadowed by arguments over who should chair the meeting.

Over the last few years, I have been in contact with the various opposition groups both inside and outside the country and have a general understanding of their aims and honest efforts. However, I have noticed a few important points through my contact with them, and ignoring them or not trying to find a solution to them, will lead to our failure, no matter how honest and dedicated we are in our struggle for a free Iran.

In my view, the main problem of the opposition groups is their old age. By old age I mean the antiquity of their ideas and their tactics.

Our opposition groups and individuals must distinguish between the old monarchical regime and the present Islamic Republic regime.

The Shah reacted to any opposition propaganda or action by trying to dismiss them or neutralise their effect through diplomatic means, but the Islamic Republic regime does, in fact, advertise its own crimes and makes no bones about its barbaric nature and regards its actions as "religious duties" and expects rewards for it. That is where we must change our tactics towards our common adversary as we are now facing a completely different regime.

Another issue for the opposition is that some of its elements or groups demand special paternalist recognition for themselves from the rest in the course of the struggle and are not prepared to sit around one table with the others or expect the rest to accept their leadership status before beginning to talk to them. For them the misery of the Iranian people under the regime comes second to their superiority amongst the opposition groups.

Today the Islamic Republic regime is like a wounded beast and has equipped itself with the latest techniques and tactics of fighting for its survival but the Iranian opposition is still adopting the tactics of 30 years ago. To win, in its struggle against the regime, the Iranian opposition must reinvent itself by bringing together the elite of our thinkers and strategists and ask them to say farewell to their personal ambitions and pride in an attempt to bring about a unity of purpose amongst our members.

Furthermore, the Iranian opposition must realise that it cannot rely on the support of the West for its objectives as they have in the last 30 years shown that they are only interested in their own national interests and not in the wellbeing or freedom of the Iranian people. We cannot blame them for this attitude, as in a free and democratic Iran, our people's interests will always come first, unlike the Islamic regime, which has put the interests of our people second to those of its regional allies.

What really should matter to the opposition groups is how they can unite around the struggle against the regime whilst avoiding divisive issues amongst themselves.

**Just as a matter of interest, can I ask you what type of relationship do you have with the former royal family of Iran? After all, they**

**are also part of the exiled opposition forces.**

_After my activities attracted the attention of our Iranian compatriots, one day Colonel Oveisi who works as an advisor to Prince Reza Pahlavi contacted me and asked me to have a meeting with the Prince with a view to cooperating with him. I went and met with him and his kind family. After our initial meeting, I used to see him on a regular basis and we always talked about many issues concerning Iran's economic conditions, its politics and its future. Together we also met with some other individuals, after which we decided to open two offices in France and America to coordinate our joint efforts, but sadly they did not last for long.

I also met with Queen Farah Pahlavi through one of our mutual friends in 2002. Later, when she decided to go to Washington to be closer to her children I arranged for the sale of her house. I still visit her from time to time and our friendship is still strong.

I have also met and become friends with Prince Ghulam Reza, the younger brother of the late Shah, through our mutual friend Dr. Aryanpour and he has stayed a while with me and my family in San Diego. All in all, our contacts and friendship are still intact.

**What do you think of the foreign countries' help to Iranians?**

_ So far, foreign countries have had a middle of the road cautious policy towards the issue of Iran. Naturally for Western governments, the interests of their own economies and people come first and so far they have shown that they are willing to live with the Islamic Republic regime if they could strike a favourable deal with it.

The presence of this destabilising regime at the heart of a volatile Middle East creates a lucrative market for Western governments to sell their arms to countries in the region and this factor makes their actions, in respect of the regime in Iran, to be different to what their words say.

I do not deny the fact that many of these Western governments have in the past condemned the actions of the regime and how it violates the human rights of our people, but at the same time some of them have also written private letters to the regime's leaders which flies in the face of their stated policies.

CHAPTER 4

# Islam in Iran

**One of the main issues of Iran is the problem if its minorities. What is your view on this issue?**

_ Minorities can be religious or class based on even political. Overall the attitude of this regime towards the people of our country is based on a serfdom relationship. Naturally as a result of this medieval thinking, our religious minorities suffer the most. I have already mentioned the historical war between the Shia and Sunni sects of Islam in Iran and how the Shia sect became the dominant religious identity of the Iranians centuries ago. It appears that throughout this history the Shia sect has been settling scores with its Sunni rival.

Despite the regime's slogans of being in favour of unity between Shias and Sunnis, it has always remained an empty slogan in the calendar of the Islamic Republic. Thirty years have passed since the Revolution and even now Sunni Iranians are not allowed to have their own mosque in Tehran to say their prayers. If this is not blatant religious discrimination, then what is? If this is the status of our Sunni citizens then you can imagine how badly other religious minorities in Iran are treated by this regime.

**But unlike the Sunnis, the Christian and Jewish Iranians do have their own churches and synagogues in Tehran as well as in other major cities.**

_ Yes and no. I say no because other religious minorities like the

Bahais are denied this right. Do you think our fellow Iranians who are Bahais can freely practise their religion? Can they even talk about their faith freely in public? Not only can they not exercise their beliefs but the regime also does not recognise them as believers at all and says their religion is a fake.

However, yes, it is true that the followers of Christianity, Judaism and Zoroastrianism have their own places of worship and do appear in them freely for prayers and congregations.

But, can they freely promote and preach their faith for others? We constantly hear about the arrest and imprisonment of newly converted Christians in Iran who have been charged with apostasy. According to the laws of the Islamic Republic regime if any citizen converts to Christianity or Judaism then they are charged as apostates and are sentenced to death.

**These newly converts must have been influenced by the missionary activities of other faiths. How can they have done it if they are not free to preach their own religions?**

_ I believe it is more the desire of the new converts to leave Islam rather than the persuasion of the missionaries that attracts them to other religions. In fact, it is the actions and deeds of the leaders of the Islamic Republic regime who regard themselves as "the actual voice of Islam" that has led many Iranians to abandon their Muslim faith.

When the Supreme Leader of this regime still regards himself as "God's representative on Earth and the Prophet's rightful successor" in the face of all the crimes his regime has committed against our people then what other reaction can you expect from the people?

When the leaders of this regime prefer their own interpretation of Islam, which secures their political and economic power and denies people their rights, freedoms and choices, then it is only natural that people will be attracted to a religion that offers them these freedoms and dignities.

In my opinion, this problem is caused by Islam becoming the system of government in Iran so that political power is justified through a faith. If another religion was doing the same and claimed legitimacy through faith and had brought so much misery to the people then it too would have suffered.

When you hide behind a religion to justify your wrongdoings then the first victim is the very religion that you are abusing. This is exactly what has happened in Iran today.

## But this negative view of Islam is not only confined to the Iranians!

_ This view of Islam is the result of the misdeeds of those who claim to be Muslims. Look at the Islam that the Taliban and Al Qaida want us to believe in! They kill humans in the name of Islam and ascribe their crimes to carrying out the words of God. Their reactionary and extremist interpretation of Islam allows them to annihilate whoever who does not think like them or side with them. The world cannot remain silent in face of the atrocities that they have committed against innocent people, especially, defenceless women and children.

It is the actions of fanatical and extremist Muslims, like the rulers of Iran that has brought about this negative view of Islam. The rulers of Iran have this illusion that they are the only Muslims in the world and only they can tell us what Islam stands for. In fact, most of the victims of these extremist Muslims are their Muslim brothers and sisters. There are many similarities between the Taliban in Afghanistan and the rulers of Iran as regards their interpretation of Islam.

I do not believe that the major religions of the world have any problem in coexisting together and showing mutual respect for each other, the inter-faith problems are caused by a minority of bigots and ignorant radicals who are the worst enemies of their own religion. The Taliban and the rulers of Iran are effectively partners in their animosity towards Islam and Islamic values despite their claims that they are the "custodians of Islam". As a Persian proverb says "you are better off to have an educated foe than an ignorant friend".

**Despite their huge population, women are also one of the minorities in Iran, what do you think of their position and the problematic issue of the obligatory hejab?**

_ Undoubtedly this is the case.

As you quite rightly say, the issue of the obligatory Islamic hejab cover for women has been a major problem for our society for many years and I believe that the guilty party here is the ruling regime.

Do the Christians, Jews or even Zoroastrians of Iran have any religious obligations to wear a hejab? The so-called anti-vice and vigilante groups have been harassing and attacking Muslims and non-Muslims on the streets of Iran for many years to enforce the hejab amongst women, ignoring the fact that their victims simply do not believe in this restriction and despise it but they cannot express their feelings about it. When they do dare to speak about the hejab and reject it, they face further repression and crackdowns from the regime's agents. The response of the ruling regime, to those women who reject the hejab, is: "you must wear it as I order you to do and if you don't like it, you must leave this country".

The regime has been following this systematic repression of our women for the last 33 years but the question is why has it not been able to succeed and why have matters become even worse in respect of the imposition of the hejab?

Why is it that many of our young Iranian women have no desire to obey this obligatory hejab and indeed ridicule the regime by doing the opposite and wearing tight clothes and deliberately showing off their hair through their scarves? Besides, is it the priority of a government, in this day and age, to engage itself in dealing with these insignificant issues? Suppose in a family, a father or mother decided to impose his or her will on their children and forced them to do things that they did not wish to do then their children would rise up in revolt against them, which is exactly what the women of Iran are doing today.

Their action to ignore and defy the compulsory hejab is a passive struggle in defence of their civil and human rights.

People choose different ways of opposing their governments in different countries. Sometimes their struggle becomes an international one for various reasons and people from other countries of the world duplicate their model of opposition. Sometimes you can find a philosophical reason for their struggle too. In Western democracies the emergence and existence of these protest groups and movements are accepted as the norm. In the West, hippies, punk rockers and heavy metal groups are part of this social phenomenon that defied the status quo and the authorities. They are more than a protest group and are looked upon as the voices of dissent against a society that ignores their aspirations and demands.

Wearing torn, filthy jeans and clothes and having long, unclean hair amongst nice and clean people wearing suits is one way of making a point or a protest.

However, the issue of the hejab for the Iranian women is not one that the world wishes to follow, as the rest of the world neither agrees with it, nor is it applicable to their own societies. In Iran itself some women look at the issue of their dress code as a means of fighting for their rights and some others just look at it as a matter of fashion preference.

**The regime justifies the imposition of the hejab cover for women as respect for their modesty and protecting moral values. In other words it claims that by covering themselves women will be immune to abuse.**

_ Then if that is true, we would not have any more cases of rape or sexual abuse against women in our country!

**But the regime says this sexual abuse is directed against those women who do not observe the hejab and, therefore, it is a good thing for them.**

_ Firstly, according to leading women's right activist, Ms Mehrangiz Caar, there is not even a proper definition of what is a good or bad hejab in Iran. The male rulers of Iran come up with one interpretation of proper or improper hejab every single day, which creates and causes more confusion in society and puts more pressure on women.

One day they say women must not wear a medium size dress. Another day they ban the wearing of long heel shoes or a certain type of boots. They cannot even make up their mind on such a simple issue that is causing so much hassle for women every single day. The reason is that the authorities do not even have any clear idea about the whole issue and their main objective is to harass and repress our women and remind them of who rules over them.

As for the regime's claim that women who do not observe the compulsory Islamic hejab stand a higher chance of being raped, this argument is completely false and nonsensical.

In the unfortunate case of a woman being raped, she is the real victim, not the rapist. After all, the rapist has not come to Iran from another planet. He is a product of this regime and has grown up under its rule. Why doesn't the regime confess to the fact that it has completely failed in educating the people of Iran on moral values and ridding society of its ills?

If I, as a father, fail to raise and educate my child to have manners and he turns into a violent person and breaks the windows of our neighbour, I cannot then blame my neighbour for the incident.

In one of his speeches before the Revolution, Khomeini told the Shah:

"Culture and the cultural education of the people is a work best done by the clergy and the religious establishment. Leave this job to us and we will show you what a decent and perfect people we shall make. If we fail to do this, then we will voluntarily accept our fault and leave the scene to others".

Nowadays every aspect of Iranian cultural, political, educational and economic life is in the hands of the clergy and their religious bodies and it is not that hard to judge the outcome of their policies and actions some 33 years after becoming the new rulers of Iran. Do

they really have the decency and courage to accept the mess they have
created in our country and leave the scene as they pledged to do? The
evidence of these 33 years proves otherwise.

**Not only non-Muslims, but even some Muslim women completely
reject or, at least, do not accept an obligatory version of the hejab.**

_ That is correct. The question of the hejab is a very complicated
and contentious issue in Islam. If you remember, the hejab did not
immediately become obligatory after the Islamic Revolution in Iran.
The new regime first ordered women employees in government
departments to observe and wear it but then later imposed it on all the
female population of the country.

In my view, here again, the regime has taken a very extreme stance
on the question of the hejab, as it has done with many other social
issues.

Is Iran the only Muslim country in the world? Even in Saudi Arabia,
which regards itself as the birthplace of Islam, wearing the hejab is
only obligatory in the two cities of Mecca and Medina and in the rest
of the country, women are free to wear it or not. In many other Muslim
countries even this level of control does not exist it all and only a
minority of women wear it and no one makes any fuss about it.

Unfortunately the ruling regime in Iran has turned an issue that
the Islamic Sharia does not even have any specific ruling on into an
absolute law, forcing and harassing women to observe it.

As far as I have researched and studied this issue, I know that
some Muslim scholars argue that even when the Koran refers to the
observance of a modest hejab cover for women; it is directed at very
religious women and not at every Muslim woman let alone non-
Muslim women.

As you know, in Islamic vocabulary, there are different descriptions
for being just a Muslim or a very devout believer. One must ask these
rulers to explain if all the women of Saudi Arabia began to observe the
hejab once the hejab verse was included in the Koran? Of course not

and the prophet did not mind at the time.

Then why are you making it an issue after many centuries today?

I doubt if the mullahs in Iran do not know these facts and it is crystal clear to everyone that they are aware of them but they just keep using the hejab issue to harass and intimidate women non-stop.

One of them argues that if Reza Shah banned the wearing of hejab by force then they should be allowed to reinstate and impose it by force too. Another extremist mullah shouts during his Friday prayers speech that blood must be shed in order to make sure that Iranian women observe the hejab properly.

I think all these comments and statements are designed to frighten Iranian people in a show of force and it is noteworthy that there is no respect for humans and their rights as a whole, regardless of whether they are women or men.

The rulers of Iran just want to remind the Iranian people that "we are here, we exist and we can always speak with you from a position of power anytime we wish to do so".

I think here we need the help of some psychiatrists to analyse the type of personality complex that these rulers suffer from. They must be suffering from a type of egoistical disease – if such a problem does exist in psychoanalysis - as they constantly and unnecessarily harass and intimidate women over such an unimportant issue that has been at the heart of the domestic policies of a regime for the last 33 years and is still unresolved. They seem to have deliberately selected women for their torturous policy. Their original excuse for imposing the hejab was that it would help bring about more modesty and virtue to society but we all know, perfectly well, that it has had disastrous and reverse effects and consequences with the women of our country being marginalised and driven out of their working and social lives.

**But it appears that Iranian women have not been marginalised and are represented in the Majles and even in the cabinet.**

_ In the discussions about the relationship between the revolution and the issue of sexuality, there are two models and if I am right this classification was first made by Valentine Moghadam.

They are the male dominated one and the version that emancipates women. In the first model, as a result of the insistence on gender differences and the role of women in the life of the family unit, women do not ultimately benefit from a social revolution.

However, in the second model the demand for sexual equality between men and women leads to greater participation for women in society, they stand to gain from that revolution.

In the first model, women are marginalised and an ideological link is created between the patriarch and the religious and nationalistic values of society. In the model, women become the main element of the family, as the family unit and its wellbeing become very important in society, even though women may have had a significant role in the success of the Revolution. But once the Revolution succeeds the State forces them into retirement and the major tasks of society are handed over to men who, in fact, then pass new legislation that cements their dominance over women.

I do not deny the presence of some women MPs in the Majles or the cabinet. But their numbers are not equal with men in terms of gender or a proportional representation of the population. If I am correct, the Iranian Majles has 290 MPs but only eight of them are women. Eight out of 290 equals to almost nothing! It is a similar story when you look at the composition of cabinet members. Let's not forget that for 30 years no woman ever held a cabinet position in Iran and even the current woman Health Minister, who was appointed to her post two years ago, has, in fact, male chauvinist views on the issue of gender equality and has issued directives for her department's staff to be segregated by sex in matters of the provision of health services to the Iranian people. Certain male doctors and specialists can no longer treat female patients; the regime has even banned them from meeting women patients.

After all, could a woman ever run for the post of President in Iran under this regime? How about becoming a member of the Assembly of Experts or the Guardian Council? Or becoming a Judge?

I do not deny the presence of women in government departments but they are all engaged in doing low-level office duties. My argument is about the way society and the State look upon the role of women in Iran.

**The same conditions for women also existed during the time of Reza Shah and Mohammad Reza Shah.**

_ That is right. I must say that although Reza Shah was interested in changing the social conditions of Iranian women at the time of his rule, he was not entirely in favour of their independent activities.

During the rule of Mohammad Reza Shah, women's rights issues were, more or less, in the realm of the government.

Despite that, women's issues and their rights were promoted by the State and many attempts were made to involve them in the social and political life of the country.

In addition, many reforms in Family Law were carried out, which granted women much more say in matrimonial affairs. Educational programs for women were launched, higher education and university courses inside and outside the country were allocated to them and for the first time ever, they were given the right to vote and be elected as Councillors, MPs and Ministers.

Gradually, the number of Iranian women holding important government posts and political positions increased, but as mentioned before, their activities were mainly controlled by the State.

During that period, despite some restrictions, much new legislation was passed through Parliament that was in support of women's rights and many other existing laws that had been based on religious and Islamic principles were either annulled or reformed. Despite all these major reforms that women benefited from, I believe that inequalities still existed in our society. This was more visible if you looked at the life of the women who lived in the rural areas of our country.

Women in the villages did not have much education and illiteracy amongst them was high. Most of them had to do low paid labour work on the farms and if they became the subject of sexual harassment or exploitation, they did not have any means of seeking justice as the law did not provide much protection for them.

These were the shortcomings and problems that our women faced then, which led to their participation in the Revolution and their siding with the religious forces against the former regime, ignoring the fact that the mullahs, and Khomeini himself, had actually opposed the limited emancipation of Iranian women and their right to vote.

Khomeini's mentor, Moddares, had publicly spoken in the Majles against the Bill that gave women the right to vote and had asked every MP to defeat it. History cannot forget their views and actions on this issue.

In his speech to the Majles, Moddares said that women must not be given the right to vote because, in his view, God created women with half a human brain and they did not have enough wisdom. He further questioned the validity of votes for women by saying "how could the women who are under the guardianship of men vote for the same men"?

In reality, our women allied themselves with this type of people and their reactionary views during the course of the Revolution and shot themselves in the foot. Immediately after the Revolution and the fall of the former regime, Iranian women were looked upon as a species whose lives must be spent at home at the service of their families where they could be mothers. This led to a considerable marginalisation of Iranian women who lost many of the rights that they had already won under the former regime.

As far as Iranian women are concerned, the victory of the Revolution has been equal to the loss of very many of the social and political rights that they had under the Shah. The new regime soon annulled the family support laws, and legalised Polygamy. I am not saying that we did not have men who had more than one wife before the

Revolution but the new regime made it legal and commonplace as it was a religious order and this was a regime that based its legitimacy on religious doctrines and ideology.

Even today Iranian women cannot travel abroad unless they have a written permission from their spouses that has been certified by a notary's office.

In 2007 a Bill was given by Iran's Ministry of Justice to the Majles for consultation under the title of "Family Support Law", Article 23 of this Bill stipulates that a man can only opt for polygamy and marry a second wife after he receives permission from a Court of Law confirming that he has enough money to maintain more than one wife and that he will make sure that he treats his wives with equal care and attention.

The Bill dropped an earlier clause that made the consent of the first wife a condition for any man who wanted to have a second wife.

It further lowered the amount of the dowry payable to divorcees and even applied heavy taxation on any funds or property that women inherited from their deceased husbands. All in all, this most anti-female, sexist and male chauvinist bill was passed despite widespread opposition from women's, and human rights', activists in Iran.

Although the Islamic Republic regime claims that it looks upon women from a humanitarian point of view and accuses the West of exploiting women as sexual objects, in reality it itself practices the opposite of what it preaches.

As you can notice, from the first day after the Revolution, the new regime tried to segregate Iranians by sex in every aspect of the nation's life, as if they carried some contagious disease between them. Even young girls were separated from boys in primary schools. Recently, there have even been proposals for sex segregation in nurseries and pre-school education centres.

I can only conclude that these acts are a reflection of the twisted minds of the rulers of this regime who are constantly thinking about sex.

Although the issue of sex segregation in the universities of Iran has resurfaced again in recent months and some universities have had to implement it, this segregation has long been in place for many years now. In university classes male students must sit in one row and female students must sit in another row behind them. The same rules apply to libraries and in some universities; there are two canteens, one for girls and another for boys.

Step out of university campuses and the story remains the same across the social life of Iranians. On buses, seats are separated for men and women. The mullahs argue this has something to do with decency and modesty as some men may harass women passengers. Even if we accept this shallow reasoning, then we need to ask ourselves why is this? Why would a man want to harass a woman on a public transport bus? Where has this man come from? What kind of society has he grown up in? Who has been responsible for teaching him manners and decency?

Why is it that since this Islamic regime has come to power, it has only managed to bring up sick and mentally disturbed individuals who are constantly thinking of harassing and abusing women?

Why do Iranian women have to pay for the weakness of the regime in controlling these mentally disturbed individuals?

If you pose these questions to the Islamic Republic regime, the answer is nearly always the same: "because they are men, they can do anything they wish to do". It is true that some of these men do get punished for their deeds but the regime's male chauvinist policies have effectively empowered men and given them a kind of freedom to satisfy their desires whilst at the same time restricting the rights of women to challenge their dominance.

Whilst this situation degrades Iranian women, it, at the same time, insults men who are looked upon by the regime as sick animals with nothing to do except intimidate and harass the opposite sex.

Despite all these social ills and the repression of the women of our country, they have not remained silent and have shown that they are capable of defending their rights and have achieved many successes under a regime that does not recognise them as equal human beings and has done nothing but erect barriers against them since its inception 33 years ago.

CHAPTER 5

# What future for the Islamic Republic?

**Some people argue that we have freedom of speech in Iran but not "the freedom of after speech".**

_ It is a painful and true irony. One must ask if we have any other form of freedom in Iran to have the freedom of speech included amongst them? In a society like Iran's, everything must complement something else. When we do not have any civil rights then to have freedom of speech next to it will sound weird. Dictatorships and tyrannical regimes are fundamentally against all types of individual and social freedoms and the Iranian regime is not an exception here.

However, let us not forget that the regime's rulers and agents have always enjoyed this exclusive freedom of speech for themselves: to say and do whatever they wish without being held accountable to anyone else.

For years, they have insulted the intelligence of our people and affronted the whole world with impunity. You may remember how the current president used the opportunity of his electioneering debate with former president Rafsanjani to dig some dirt on him and his family and publicly insult them on national television. But the same president cannot even listen, let alone accept the slightest constructive criticism and will respond harshly and accuse his critics of insulting him and the "honourable leader". Then he so unashamedly claims in an interview with an American reporter that: "Iran is the most democratic country of the world where everyone can express their opinions without fear".

In a way, he is not lying because once anyone expresses his or her opinion they will automatically lose their freedom afterwards. In fact, Ahmadinejad cleverly avoids talking about the consequences of a person speaking his or her mind and regards his statement as factual, and that he is telling the truth, which is nothing more than a self-deception.

The blind admirers of the Supreme Leader have made him virtually an inaccessible man so that any complaints made to him, such as by a group of Iran's political prisoners writing an open letter about the harsh and inhumane conditions in their prisons, would be as if one was "waging war on a Saint or God himself" and that the blood of the protestors must be shed for this "Sin".

In the Assembly of Experts, one member was naïve enough to say that the Supreme Leader had discarded Justice as a qualification of being the Leader of the Revolution and was immediately told to shut up and later on, he was dismissed!

Look at the raids on the homes of some of the most revered grand ayatollahs who did not agree with Khamenei on his direct support of bringing Ahmadinejad into power. Gangs of pro-government thugs attacked their homes, ransacked their offices and beat their supporters savagely and what did Mr. Khamenei do to protect the rights of those senior ayatollahs? Nothing! He did not even raise an eyebrow for this most unprecedented violation against Iranian religious leaders in the history of Islam. Yet the regime's yes men mullahs all claim that Iran and the Islamic Republic is ruled by "the most noble and just ayatollah of all time"!

At the same time, some people and state organs that enjoy the backing of certain influential interest groups, can say anything and smear anyone they dislike or oppose with complete impunity. For many years the Kayhan daily has been the mouthpiece of Khamenei and the paper's so-called editor openly insults and humiliates whoever he wants and no one dares to sue him for his defamatory articles. He has repeatedly been cleared of all the slander charges brought against him and the paper. He continues to defame and humiliate anyone who dares to say or do anything that questions the Supreme Leader's decisions.

Nobody dared to sue the mullah who said in his sermon that Ahmadinejad's chief of staff is "his reproductive organ"! Another mullah who openly called for the assassination of Rahim Mashaie, Ahmadinejad's right hand man, has never been questioned by any law enforcement body in the country. The mullah in fact said in his sermon that he would be personally responsible for the payment of the bounty and that God had blessed the act of killing Mashaie!

Now compare this "freedom" for the regime's rulers and supporters to do and say anything they wish with impunity, with the cases of hundreds of innocent journalists, students and civil rights activists who have been jailed for making a civilised, constructive and light criticism of the regime's domestic or foreign policies.

Only very recently a young woman student who is doing her doctorate degree at the University of Tehran was flogged 70 times on charges of "insulting the President". Reacting to public outrage about the incident Ahamdinejad claimed that he had never complained against anyone and did not even know the woman! This goes to show the two tier system of justice that exists in today's Iran where the population does not trust a judicial system that is nothing more than a tool of repression in the hands of the rulers.

Whilst these types of miscarriages of justice are commonplace in Iran, in advanced and democratic countries, such an incident would have led to the fall or resignation of the government as every citizen, whether an ordinary worker or a Prime Minister, respects the law of the land and relics on an independent justice system that protects everyone's rights regardless of their position, race, beliefs or gender.

But in today's Iran, no journalist, writer, blogger and intellectual have any security at all and as our national poet Saadi said many centuries ago "our rulers have chained us and unleashed the dogs".

The moment one tries to follow a piece of news, or subject of national interest, one makes oneself available to intimidation and imprisonment. Then when you complain about the lack of justice, the Supreme Leader orders you to shut up and stop interfering with the judicial system!

How many dailies and publications have been closed down in the last few years?

It is interesting that they have all been shut down on the same charges of "disturbing public opinion", "acting against national security", "spreading lies" or "insulting the President or the Leader".

The way they crackdown on dissidents and stifle citizens' civil and human rights is identical to what dictators like Stalin did. It must come as no surprise that hundreds of thousands of Iranians still continue to leave the country and live in exile.

In the case of the recent massive $3 billion fraud at the Central Bank, the Supreme Leader told the media "not to make much noise about this issue and allow the justice system to do its job". He deliberately forgets that, in fact, it was because of the silence of the Iranian media, and the crackdown on independent newspapers, that such an astronomical embezzlement was able to take place in the country's banking system! No one could expect the Majles and its deputies to investigate this unprecedented fraud and bring the culprits to justice as they are nothing more than lick spittles in a rubber stamp parliament who are only good at heaping praises on the Supreme Leader and his acolytes.

## What kind of Society do we get under these circumstances?

_ A closed society where the whims of a dictator dominate all its social, political and cultural life whilst censorship and tyranny rule over its citizens.

Nobody is safe in this society except those who wield political and economic power whilst intellectuals, writers, filmmakers, actors, lawyers and anyone capable of thinking differently is in danger of persecution.

This situation leads to the collapse of all cultural and moral values and corruption dominates every aspect of the nation's existence. When you deny citizens their freedom of thought and imprison those who have dared to do so then fear rules over society and you either have to run away and survive or stay and accept the loss of your human rights. Under such circumstances, criminals "prosper" and criminality hides itself behind hypocrisy and pretentious behaviour. In short, individual and social norms and values take a dip into the abyss.

Those who cracked down on our people in the post-election disturbances had not come to our country from another planet. They had been bred inside this vile political and cultural atmosphere that the regime had created. They were people whose only source of information and knowledge were the propaganda devices of a tyrannical regime who had ordered them to crackdown on their own brothers and sisters and fellow countrymen and women.

To this day some of them still claim that Neda was killed in a conspiracy organised by the British government because they have been brainwashed by the lying machine that is the Islamic Republic regime.

**How do you assess the book publishing market situation in Iran?**
_ The Islamic Republic regime claims that it has always supported the promotion of cultural and scientific activities but the reality of the situation in the world of publishing in Iran tells us that the average print run of books is around 2,000 copies. In the field of philosophy, it is simply a disastrous situation indeed. Books about philosophical discourse are only printed in book runs of less than a 1,000 copies.

These are disastrous statistics and one must ask these gentlemen to answer why, when they claim to be supportive of cultural activities, does the country have such a low rate of book readers per capita?

Those independent writers or publishing houses that dare to spend a great deal of time and money to put together a title must first hand it over to the censorship office of the Ministry of Culture for permission to publish it. Hundreds of such titles have been gathering dust in the ministry's basements for years.

When the authors ask for explanations they are told that they should not complain as the same system of censorship and certification existed before the Revolution. Then one needs to ask these agents of tyranny what was the purpose of making that Revolution and going through so much bloodshed and destruction in the country if we are back to where we were 33 years ago?

**Could the high price of books have anything to do with the low number of book readers in Iran?**

_ In comparison with other commodities, the price of books in the markets is not that high. A major cause of the problem of the low number of book readers in Iran is the lack of interest amongst the population. People are so tied up with running their daily lives and making ends meet that they are left with little or no time to relax and spend some time reading books.

I believe the Iranian regime has deliberately made life difficult for people so as to keep them busy so that they will not bother it.

Under despotic regimes, when you occupy people's minds with how they are to survive from day to day then they will not have the time to think about virtues like liberty and democracy.

On the contrary, in democratic societies governments try to keep their people happy and prosperous to keep them quiet and not bother the authorities.

**How do you see the issue of censorship in Iran?**

_ I have mentioned it before that this regime looks upon the Iranian people as its serfs. It regards itself as the guardian of the people. In the field of ideology, the regime is only interested in imposing its own school of thoughts and dogmas on the people. It tells people what to read, how to think, what to watch, what to wear and so on and so forth.

The banning of satellite dishes that receive foreign broadcast programs must be seen in this context. The regime is so weak in its ideology that it cannot even tolerate how people view things in their private lives and so it infringes on the most private affairs of its own citizens.

If the rulers of Iran had the slightest decency, they would publicly confess to the fact that they have completely failed in implementing their own cultural values, which are based on the complete obedience of the populace to the regime's orders.

They must realise that the era of Stalinist policies has long since passed and that it cannot make people become religious or believers in the ideology it pushes on them by force.

For many years, Iranians have been paying a heavy price for the wrong policies, in domestic and international issues, of the regime that rules over them.

The regime conceals its failures in the management of the country by repressing the people. The Iranian people never receive any truthful news from their national radio and TV broadcasting organisations and are constantly fed a diet of lies and deceit.

Many people dislike the output of these media organisations that are run on the basis of producing propaganda material for the regime and sycophantic coverage of the leader who personally selects the head of the national broadcasting organisation so what does the regime expect the people to do?

Would they not then turn to the foreign and satellite stations for news and entertainment programs? The regime cannot even tolerate this limited freedom of choice for the people and removes and dismantles satellite dishes from the roofs of homes and jams foreign satellite broadcasting to Iran. The forbidden fruit is always sweeter as they say and once the regime resorts to all these repressive measures, the thirst of the Iranian people to tune into satellite programs becomes greater than ever before.

Today you can see an element of force and the state's approval in every aspect of the cultural life of Iran. History has proved that neither this type of state manufactured culture nor the authoritarian ideologies behind it are sustainable. How can you censor a book that has existed for several hundred years and change its contents and tell people they must only read those chapters that the government approves of? This is the case with the Khosrow and Shirin Love Story Book, which has existed for nearly a thousand years in our rich literature. The regime has ordered publishers that the book may be reprinted only when certain love poems have been deleted from the original version because they are "very intimate conversations between two lovers"! Have all the many thousands of our people who have read this classic over many centuries been corrupted by reading these love poems?

The mullahs have suddenly found out that these poems are "harmful" to the cultural values of Iranians and can corrupt their minds. Iranian cultural values are, in fact, deeply rooted in the love stories of its literature. The outside world knows Iranians through their Persian poetry of love stories and fables more than anything else. This way of looking at culture and its foundations can only be the product of a sick mind that has no comprehension of human nature and desires.

Besides, the mullahs ruling Iran, close their eyes the moral corruption amongst their own sort, why don't they order the closure of the religious seminaries where many cases of corruption take place every single day?

The regime has taken the censorship of books to unprecedented levels by even distorting our recorded history the way it would like to represent it. The Supreme Leader has advised people not to read the pre-Islamic history of Iran and only study our history after the Arabs conquered Iran.

Why should people do this?

What does the regime gain from its anti-Iranian stance?

Why does the regime have so much animosity for Iran and Iranians?

**The regime has actually removed the history of Iranian kingdoms and dynasties from the school curriculum.**

_ Sadly that is true but I believe this decision reflects their fear of Iranian nationalism. They are doing their best to cut off our people from their past history. They just want the people to think that our history only began with the arrival of the Mullahs' regime on the scene.

I don't deny the achievements of Iran under the rule of Islam. One cannot deny the emergence of great Iranian poets and philosophers like Omar Khayam, Avecina, Abu Rayhan, Farabi and Kahje Nassir.

But how could you so easily ignore the contribution of Cyrus the Great to the old civilisation?

History is not just for reading. It is a channel that links us to our roots and tells us who we are and where we have come from. If I don't know who my ancestors are and what historic background I was born into then I have no roots to anything and this spirit of alienation is what that the regime wants to spread amongst our people in order to rule over them easily.

The regime's double standards clearly show that it is not honest with the Iranian people and is always engulfed in contradictions. Whilst the regime keeps talking about the so-called "cultural invasion of foreign powers on Iran", at the same time, it stifles the natural and national culture of the country through repressive measures.

The regime is constantly in fear of people and their knowledge and keeps misleading them with deceitful information. It just doesn't want to accept that the time that authoritarian regimes could create an iron curtain around their borders and stop their people from communicating with the outside world has long since passed.

**Let me ask you about Iranian cinema. Do you follow the artistic creations made in Iran?**

_ Naturally due to my occupation and my very busy work schedule, I cannot follow Iranian cinema as an art critic but I do watch Iranian films and follow the news of the Iranian film industry. It appears that Iranian cinema is not faring any better than the world of publishing under this regime. In fact, the problems of the Iranian cinema industry are far greater as production costs are higher than book publishing and many directors and filmmakers are tempted to make low budget and amateurish feature films.

Maybe we should talk more about the regime's policies in the film industry rather than Iranian cinema, as my knowledge of Iranian films is very limited.

I believe that whatever problems that do exist in the area of artistic creations in Iran, whether in cinema, book publishing and the general culture of the country, are a direct consequence of the regime's policies that are being implemented through a group of unqualified managers who were appointed for their loyalty to the regime rather than for being an expert in the field of their chosen profession.

It appears that under this regime, everyone is a jack of all trades, overnight; a cleric can become a politician and an expert on international affairs. A police commander can appear as a preacher of Islamic verses in the middle of a community meeting. Likewise, someone whose background is murky and no one knows if he has even gone to a movie house to watch a film becomes a member of the jury in one of the regime's many film festivals! It should not be that difficult to assess the impact of these people's views and actions on the cultural life of Iran.

The regime installs uneducated and unprofessional people who obey its directives to manage various government departments and public offices. They remain in their undeserved jobs until such a day that they completely destroy the effectiveness of their departments and then they are moved into other posts to do the same all over again!

It may be that individuals are not to be blamed for this mismanagement of the country's affairs but certainly they are guilty of not admitting to their lack of expertise and inexperience and of accepting any jobs that are given to them in return for their loyalty to the regime, jobs that should have gone instead to educated and professional men and women. This effectively means that the system is flawed. When clerics, whose understanding of politics and running the economic and social life of a country is equal to zero, are put charge of the nation then we must expect to end up in situation like this.

The clerical regime in Iran has mistaken the task of managing a country with running the affairs of a local mosque or religious foundation.

You cannot run a country on the basis of trial and error. The vast sphere of the government and its many departments cannot depend on one leader or manager for its proper functioning. It has to be run by teams of professionals and experts as in today's modern and fast moving world many old and centralised departments are broken down into smaller, specialist units but the clergy in Iran regards themselves as being the "source of imitation and reference" for all social, political, economic and cultural matters of the nation.

If you look at the contents of the speeches of the Supreme Leader you will notice that his vocabulary is always packed with advisory comments as if he is the ultimate expert in matters ranging from the country's economic problems to the style of poetry and film script writing. Naturally this closed system of government will not allow elite and professional people to enter state bodies, as the undeserved position of its own ineffective subordinates would then be untenable.

The irony of this situation is that the country spends millions of dollars every year to educate hundreds of thousands of young men and women in various fields of social sciences, medicine, engineering and so on but they are not absorbed by the government for the reasons already mentioned, most of them end up leaving Iran and offering their hard achieved expertise to foreign countries. This regime is unique in wasting the natural and human resources of our country at a colossal rate.

**So you do believe that there is a brain drain amongst Iran's**

**educated elite?**

_ Yes, that is exactly what is happening in our country. Usually in Iranian airports the security and airline staff check that no one attempts to take any banned or unauthorised valuables out of the country but they all fail to see the loss of far greater items of national treasures, the minds of our educated elite, are leaving the country and are going for ever. Many of these experts and professionals who have left Iran will never come back once they experience the security and social freedoms that they enjoy in foreign countries.

Just imagine if hundreds of thousands of people, like me, were to go back to our own Motherland and offer our skills, wealth, creativity and entrepreneurship to the development of the country then imagine what major changes would take place there overnight!

Sadly, the conditions for this to happen are not there. There is no security for any capital or industrial investment in Iran. Investors would never risk entering any venture in Iran under current circumstances.

The country is not run on the principles of national interests and does not have any economic stability.

CHAPTER 6

# Iran and the Arab Spring

**Let's talk about the issues of the region and the social revolutions that are taking place and are known as the Arab Spring. What do you think lies behind these events in countries like Egypt?**

_ Many factors have contributed to the current revolution in Egypt. The most important of them are the economic, social and religious factors and the presence of a united opposition.

All these factors except the united opposition make the Egyptian revolution look identical to the rise of the current freedom movement in Iran.

**But most of these factors exist in many countries of the world. Why haven't they had a revolution as well?**

_ Yes, you're right, but apart from the existence of these factors you need to add in a people's desire and will for change, plus international support to launch a movement. These factors may exist in many countries of the world, including Iran, but they are not backed by the overwhelming will of the people for change and they lack international support

For example, after the rigged presidential elections in Iran in 2009, the regime rounded up thousands of people and cracked down on the pro-democracy movement and eventually managed to silence the protestors. It even tolerated opposition figures like Mousavi and Karoubi for a year or so and finally put them under house arrest and again silenced the movement by using repression.

All this happened as the world stood by and watched the crackdown of the freedom movement at the hands of the regime because world powers prefer this radical and subversive regime to survive and cause instability in the region so that they can sell their arms to the countries that neighbour Iran.

The amount of armaments that the countries neighbouring Iran have bought since 2009 is unprecedented.

In the meantime, Mousavi and Karoubi have sent their spokesmen abroad to meet media organisations in the Free World who are interested in broadcasting their views as it seems that they want to keep this regime in power with certain cosmetic changes to its policies.

It is true that many responsible leaders of the Free World have condemned the crimes of the Islamic Republic regime against the people of Iran, but at the same time, some of them have also written personal letters to the Leader of this despotic regime as they consider, in their calculations, that the existence of the regime is beneficial, even though this position is against the natural interests of the Iranian people.

**Do you see any similarities between the democracy movements in Iran and Egypt?**

_ Yes, although Egypt was in a relatively better economic shape than Iran, several factors made its economy look similar to Iran's. First and foremost, is its public sector. In the public sector, the government becomes so big and interferes in every aspect of the country's economic and political life, if we add the authoritarian tendencies of big government that usually follow these interventions, then we have a recipe for public dissatisfaction. The problem of unemployment amongst the young and educated people and rising inflation makes the matter worse.

In certain ways, the Iranian regime has been taking advantage of the Egyptian revolution because of the involvement of the Muslim

Brotherhood amongst the opposition forces that ousted the Mubarak regime.

Egypt has always had a very large rural population who have, by and large, remained very traditional and religious in their social and political views.

One must not forget Egypt's important role in recent years in the Arab-Israeli peace process. The Muslim Brotherhood had long opposed the former regime's involvement in this process and this led the peasantry to join the anti-government forces and speed up the course of the revolution.

The Iranian regime has capitalised on this factor and claims that the Egyptian revolution is based on its own Islamic Revolution. By doing this, Tehran has been trying to influence Egyptian Muslims into duplicating the Islamic Republic as the model for their next government.

However, Muslim and secular groups along with the followers of other religions in Egypt have rejected the Iranian leader's claims and made it clear that the next Egyptian government will be based on what the people of Egypt decide and it is entirely up to them and not to a foreign country, as to what type of government they would like to have in the future.

In my view, the Iranian leadership knows very well that the Egyptian revolution is very different to what happened in Iran 33 years ago but that it is pushing its luck. In fact by trying to poach the Egyptian revolution, the Iranian regime has been doing its best to cover up its own failures in Iran, especially the tarnished and disgraceful images that the whole world saw after its bloody crackdown on the Iranian people following the 2009 rigged elections.

Whilst Tehran has been trying to show off its supposed power to export its Islamic revolution to other countries, the Egyptian people have shown that they are mature enough not to fall into this trap which replaces one form of tyranny with another and they have made it clear that their struggle is for the establishment of Democracy.

**But in Tunisia the conditions were somehow different. The government of Zeinulabedin Bin Ali carried out the economic reforms that were proposed by the International Monetary Fund and the World Bank and it appeared that he had, to some extent, succeeded in bringing an economic boom to his country but the Tunisian people still rose up in revolt against him and his government. How would you analyse the Tunisian revolution?**

_ The issues that you have mentioned are quite true. However, in my view Tunisia suffered from the problems of an imbalanced economic growth. In addition to this, the country had not fully achieved political maturity.

In reality, all these economic reforms had taken place within a closed and dictatorial political system. It was as if you wanted to install a Mercedes Benz engine into a second-hand cheap car. Naturally they will not function properly as politics and the economy are the two inseparable foundations of every society and they either grow together or do not.

During Bin Ali's era, no political parties or trade union organisations were allowed to operate. The Tunisian people did not have any freedom of speech or association, as is the case with all the countries that are ruled by tyrannical regimes, including today's Iran.

When you gag your people and deny them the right to speak their minds then you have to expect that one day they will revolt against you in order to vent decades of suppressed feelings and aspirations.

Bin Ali did eventually tell the Tunisian people that he had heard their voice but it was too little and too late to save him and his regime.

I have absolutely no doubt that this same scenario will happen in Iran too and that the ruling regime will one day hear the voice of Iranians but will not survive their wrath.

It is very strange that history keeps repeating itself but no one seems to be learning any lesson from it. What strange species we humans are!

Along with a closed political system, Tunisia never had any

transparent economic system either.

People were suffering from a lack of social justice and as we all know the revolution started when a young peddler set himself on fire in public as a protest against his economic conditions. When he died, the police confiscated the little property that he had and the people rose up in fury. The fate of Bin Ali's regime was then sealed at the hands of the Tunisian people.

Bin Ali's economic policies had effectively widened the gap between the rich and the poor in Tunisia. Only a handful of his cronies could benefit from the wealth of the nation and the rest were just eeking out a day by day existence.

High unemployment was another factor in Bin Ali's downfall. I read in a report that the young peddler, who publicly burnt himself to death, was actually an educated man who had not been able to find a job after university and had to sell stuff on the streets in order just to survive. When the educated classes face the problem of unemployment, their reaction will be quite conscious and different from those of the rest of society.

You can see this in the way they have used the Internet to make their revolutionary voice heard.

This means that the educated elites have acted as the engines of the protest movements and that they are now a new class of people who belong to the cyber generation.

The peasantry and the working class may have joined the democratic movements in the Arab world but the educated elites have been at the vanguard of those movements. Naturally, being educated and rational, they put forward many reasonable and realistic demands that attracted people towards them rather than to Bin Ali's promises of reform.

The opposition to Bin Ali consisted of many people who had the power of analysing the developments properly. From this point of view, I believe the Tunisian opposition movement is identical to Iran's freedom movement. No wonder after Bin Ali's fall, the protestors on the streets of Iran were shouting slogans against Ali Khamenei and likening his dictatorship to that of Bin Ali's.

If we add the corruption of Bin Ali's family to all these issues, where they had become the ruling family that was plundering the wealth of Tunisia, then the recipe for a revolution becomes complete.

**Why is it that the Iranian regime supports the Arab Spring in every Arab country except Syria?**

_ Sadly, in today's world, money and material interests have the final say in international politics. The Russian and Chinese governments use their veto power in the UN to support the Assad regime simply because his despotic and repressive regime benefits them financially.

For the Chinese and Russian governments, the issue of human rights comes second to the survival of a brutal regime that looks after their interests in the region. Effectively, by using their veto to derail the UN resolutions on the Assad regime, Moscow and Beijing have closed their eyes to the daily massacre of the Syrian people by one of the most tyrannical regimes in the Middle East.

This is exactly what they have done in respect of the crimes of the Islamic Republic regime against the people of Iran.

The Russians and the Chinese have agreed economic sanctions on Iran in order to avoid criticism against themselves, knowing very well that the Iranian people will suffer from these sanctions but that the rulers of Iran, as their trade partners, will ultimately share the profits with Moscow and Beijing.

The Iranian rulers' support for the Assad regime is very eye-opening, but it was not unexpected. The Islamic Republic regime has somehow tied up its existence to anti-Israeli policies and will go to any length to try to prove to the world that it will one day defeat the Israelis.

The Syrian regime has been the Islamic Republic's staunchest ally in this crusade and the Iranian regime will naturally do anything to sustain Assad in power.

In reality, from the point of view of the Iranian regime, the criteria of being right or wrong depends on how much a democratic movement allies itself with the policies of the Mullahs' regime in Iran.

The regime, hypocritically, supports the Palestinian people against Israeli policies towards them, but Arab people are denied even the slightest sympathy when they are being massacred by the Assad regime!

Politics aside, the Iranian regime does not even practise the most basic principle of Islam, which teaches its followers to come to the aid of fellow Muslims when they are being suppressed by their rulers.

Unfortunately, the Syrian people are suffering from the same problems as the Iranians and that is that they are ruled by a regime whose priorities are not the interests of their own people but how to meddle in disputes between other nations.

For years, the Iranian regime has made the Palestinian-Israeli conflict a scapegoat for its own failures at home and made the protection of the interests of extremists in Palestine, Lebanon, Afghanistan and even Venezuela, the basis of its foreign policy.

## What role have the Internet and social networks played in these democratic movements?

_ There is no doubt that we now live in a world that is dominated by the power of information technology and cyberspace. This has led to our social actions becoming global. Social networks and the Internet have given new meanings and dimensions to the values of democracy and freedom.

Although different countries may have different cultural values and traditions, the freedoms offered by mass communications have helped them to get closer to each other in pursuit of shared values and principles. This is what Marshal McLohan has referred to as "Globalisation".

The Internet has effectively reduced the power of dictators, as the moment they commit a crime against their victims, it will be broadcast around the world. It may not stop them from committing their crimes, but it has certainly blunted their swords to some extent.

I say, to some extent, because at the end of the day, it is through the will and power of the people that dictators will be deposed and their tyranny replaced with democracy and prosperity for the people.

It should come as no surprise that regardless of their nationality, all the despots of the world are united in their dislike of the Internet and social networks as well as satellite channels and do their best to filter the Internet and jam the satellite programs beamed into their countries.

**Do you think, as American political leaders have said, that the breeze of democracy in the Middle East, which began in Tehran's Freedom Square will once again return to its birthplace?**

_ Undoubtedly! We have an expression in Persian that says "a country run on blasphemy may survive but it will surely collapse under repression".

Iranian rulers have deceitfully depicted the Arab Spring as being a by-product of the Islamic Revolution and refer to it as the "Islamic Awakening".

However, behind their comments about the democratic movements that have swept the Middle East, one can easily detect their fear of the tide reaching Iranian shores, where it all started three years ago and that day is, certainly, not too far away.

In my view, Western governments still benefit from the regime's existence and its use by date has not entirely passed, when that date does arrive, then just like the Saddam regime, the Islamic Republic will face its own eventual downfall. I noticed this, in President Obama's views on Iran, and believe, if we read between the lines of his comments, that we can well see this scenario.

**Thank you for your valuable time on this interview.**

_ Thank you in return.

Articles and Commentaries

# The people of Iran are not the same as the ruling regime

When Iranian President, Mahmoud Ahmadinejad, attended the annual session of the United Nations General Assembly in New York five years ago, the American media, which usually looks for sensational topics in order to attract a wider audience, gave great coverage to the address by this new president whose aim was to succeed the revolutionary leaders of the second part of the Twentieth Century such as "Nasser" – prompting him to speak of wiping Israel off the map and changing the world order. The newspapers printed his picture and his pretentious comments on their front page. The American people had their first introduction to a man whose superiority complex had prompted him to place himself at the same level as the likes of Roosevelt, Stalin and Mao, whilst the ruling leaders in his own country did not take him seriously.

Meanwhile, the producers of many prominent television programmes such as Larry King were competing to get an interview with Ahmadinejad. They knew that his comments would be funny and entertaining and would attract a large audience.

In the same year, Hugo Chavez, who equalled his friend, Ahmadinejad, in delivering long speeches and speaking nothing but utter nonsense, also attended the annual session of the UN General Assembly. I wrote an article, which was published by the Washington Post. In it, I analysed their situations and positions amongst their respective people.

I, especially, highlighted the fact that Ahmadinejad and the others who currently rule Iran do not represent the Iranian people and the views that they express at the General Assembly or to the news media are not acceptable to the people.

Today, the truth of those comments, made all those years ago, have now become evident to the international media and the leaders of Western countries, especially the United States and the Great Britain. Today, the leaders, the politicians and those who live in the West have come to realise that Iranian people, like those living in  developed countries,  pursue freedom and democracy because not only have they gained greater political and social consciousness but also because they have fought for democracy and paid the price by being jailed, tortured, or sent into exile. Today, the world knows that the despotic religious regime, the ruling Ayatollahs, the junior and senior officials in Iran blatantly oppose democracy, freedom and human rights. They silence the voices and cries of freedom. We also remember that the president of Columbia University described Ahmadinejad as a "petty dictator", before the Iranian president delivered a speech full of lies and deception at that university. Not long afterwards, Ahamdinejad's claim that Iran was the "freest country in the world" was ridiculed by politicians and the mass media.

It is also important to view the difference between the Iranian people and those who rule the country from another angle. Since the tragic events of September 11, 2001 which caused the deaths of over 3,000 people and plunged thousands of families into deep mourning, the leaders of the Islamic Republic have not condemned this act of terrorism and have failed to offer any words of sympathy to either the families who were affected or the American people.

On the contrary, they have manufactured mad and outrageous fantasies, blatantly accusing government agencies in the US of being responsible for this tragic event – thereby, adding salt to the injury. In contrast, the Iranian people reacted with a great heart-felt, sympathetic and civilised behaviour.

Defying the prevalent oppressive and frightening atmosphere in the streets of Tehran - where the regime used any excuse to crackdown on gatherings of any sort - hundreds of men and women held a candle light vigil on the evening of September 11 in Mohseni Square to offer their sympathy to the families in mourning and to the American people. That action prompted American politicians to distinguish between the Iranian people and those who rule the country.

Former US president, George W. Bush, referred to this issue many times in his speeches. President Obama - who sincerely tried to end the animosities with the Iranian regime but instead encountered a violent response from the leaders in Tehran – on many occasions, particularly in his Nowruz message of two years ago, highlighted the difference between the Iranian people and those running the country.

Ahmadinejad has given interviews to the US media during his visits to that country. He was interviewed by Charlic Rose, the prominent broadcast journalist. He freely spoke his mind during the interview, blatantly attacking the US and Western officials. He expressed his – hostile and medieval – views without any restrictions or obstructions. By now he must have understood that expressing one's view without fear is one of the benefits of democracy and freedom of speech, something that the Iranian people are entitled to, but have been deprived of.

The annual session of the UN General Assembly provides an exceptional opportunity to world leaders to present their views to other leaders and the billions of people around the globe who watch these proceedings very closely.

The presidents and prime ministers who attend the session of the UN General Assembly try to take advantage of this rare opportunity to discuss the issues concerning their respective countries with other world leaders – either during their addresses to the UN General Assembly or talks held on the sidelines of the formal session – and find solutions to those problems. This year, we witnessed how Mahmoud Abbas, President of the Palestinian National Authority, took advantage of this opportunity and presented his historical proposal for the formation of an independent Palestine, thereby receiving praise and support from the majority of world leaders. At the other corner, Israeli Prime Minister Benjamin Netanyahu- whether one agrees with his views or not – tried to gain support for his views by highlighting the national interests of his country.

In the past seven years, Ahmadinejad has been the only leader who despite his lengthy addresses has failed to speak about Iran's national interest; instead he has used his turn to speak to launch violent diatribes on Western leaders, generating animosity against Iran and the very regime which he represents. Ahmadinejad's comments and his position on world matters have brought nothing but sanctions against Iran, pushing the country further into isolation.

In his address to the session of the UN General Assembly this year, Ahmadinejad again spoke about many irrelevant issues except the problems concerning Iran and its people. Apart from his brazen lecturing of other world leaders on moral and leadership matters and his prophetic promises on the advent of the twelfth Shia Imam [Mahdi] who will bring peace and justice to the world, Ahmadinejad, this year, added the First and Second World War to the list of topics which already included the September 11 tragedy and the refutation of Holocaust, and laid wholesale blame on Western leaders, especially those in the US, for every tragedy and disaster that has occurred in the past two centuries.

Whilst Ahmadinejad speaks of world leadership and wishes to be a player on the global stage, he has, at the same time, plunged the country into poverty and despair, fuelled internal political disputes and been unable to tackle domestic issues such as collecting taxes and eliminating subsidies.

Will the problems that currently face Iran be resolved if Ahmadinejad were to succeed in proving his claims regarding the Holocaust, September 11 and the First and Second World War?

How does discussing Guantanamo Bay and the violation of human rights in America and Europe help to tackle the issues facing Iran? There is no doubt that highlighting such issues – and conspicuously excluding Russia and China from his comments – is just a ploy to shift blame and cover up the Islamic Republic's managerial incompetence, ineffectiveness, despotism and oppressive rule. Incidentally, shortly after Ahmadinejad spoke – again - about September 11 at this year's session of the UN General Assembly, blaming the US for the tragedy, the terrorist network Al-Qaida issued a statement, asking Ahmadinejad to stop theorising about September 11. In its statement, Al-Qaida, once again claimed responsibility for September 11, describing it as a heroic act. The statement said that the Islamic Republic considers Al-Qaida as its competitor, because it is well aware of the wide influence that this network exerts in the region. It aims to tarnish Al-Qaida's reputation by ascribing responsibility for September 11 to the US!

On the other hand, Ahmadinejad's address to this year's session of the UN General Assembly clearly revealed that any claim by the Iranian regime to support the demands of the Palestinian people is just empty rhetoric. The Iranian president allocated a segment of his annual address to the issue of Palestine. However, he did not lend his support to Mahmoud Abbas's proposal for an independent Palestine after the latter presented his proposal to the UN General Assembly. A week later, the leader of the regime publically expressed his opposition to the plan, which had received the approval of the Palestinians.

The truth is that the Islamic Republic system is hated by the Iranian people due to the oppressive atmosphere it has created inside Iran.

Its antagonistic policies and actions have caused it to be further isolated from the international community. Also, it has no footing amongst the countries in the region.

Iranian people long for democracy and freedom inside the country. They wish to establish cordial and friendly relationships with all the countries in the world; those in the region, Europe and the US. They wish to live in peace and harmony with the rest of the world.

Iranians have taken big and effective steps towards achieving democracy, freedom and finding a respectable place for themselves amongst the international family of nations. They will eventually achieve their goals.

# A behavioural study of the leaders of the Islamic Republic

A study into the behaviour and actions of the leaders of the Islamic republic reveals certain patterns that repeat themselves with some frequency. To illustrate this point, we'll analyse Ahmadinejad's recent interview with a CNN reporter. Other issues such as the US were discussed in this interview; however, we leave it to others to analyse those remarks. For our purposes, we'll focus on the topic of this chapter.

## A) Sophistry

One of Ahmadinejad's major problems is how he confuses his explanations and interpretations of the issues. Ahmadinejad gave an interesting answer when asked by the interviewer about the extent of Iran's presence in Iraq after the withdrawal of the US military from the country. He said: "Iran and Iraq have always held a special and historical relationship. The two nations have shared a strong historical, cultural and religious bond. Therefore, the presence or absence of the American troops will have no impact on the special and historical relationship between the two countries."

Highlighting the cordial and friendly ties between the Islamic Republic of Iran and the government, Council of Representatives and various political parties in Iraq, Ahmadinejad described the relationship between the two countries as deep and wide and said: "The existence of various holy sites in Iraq and the relationship between religious scholars and leaders have strengthened the ties between Iran and Iraq. There are not many countries in the world which hold such strong ties. Even the war that was instigated by Saddam against Iran– with the support of the West – failed to interfere with the relationship between the two countries."

It is astonishing how he confuses and misuses words. Clearly the question was about the presence of the Iranian government in Iraq not the people. However, Ahmadinejad - intentionally or unwittingly - replaces people for the government, so that he can claim that there is no difference between the people and the government. In other words, they are a single soul occupying two bodies. Therefore, Iran and Iraq enjoy strong ties because the Shia scholars, religious centres and holy sites are in that country. Although, Ahmadinejad does not clarify whether he means the government or the people when he speaks of Iran and Iraq, his statement, however, about the relationship between the two countries - even in relation to the war - shows that he means the people, because the animosity between the two governments during the war clearly does not need to be substantiated.

Ahmadinejad tries to paint an impartial portrait of Iran when it comes to Iraq's affairs. That is why he claims that the Islamic Republic holds cordial and friendly ties with the government, Council of Representatives and the various political parties in Iraq. However, existing facts and Iran's support for special groups prove otherwise. By merging the people and the government together, Ahmadinejad gives a misleading answer to the question about the government, in other words, he does not answer the question.

We can witness this confusion at another point in the interview. Ahmadinejad said: "We believe that the current – imposed - problems and obstacles have been caused by Western pressure and interference. There wouldn't be any problems amongst the countries in the region – especially between Iran and Saudi Arabia - if these pressures didn't exist. Over one million Iranians travel to Saudi Arabia annually. The relationship between the two countries is friendly and cordial." What do one million Iranians travelling to Saudi Arabia have anything to do with the relationship between the two countries? Iran has never prevented pilgrims from visiting Saudi Arabia despite the bad treatment Iranian pilgrims have received in recent years in that country. Even if the Saudis were to treat the Iranian pilgrims well, we still couldn't base the relations between the countries on this issue. Saudi Arabia views Iranian pilgrims as tourists, people who can help that country's economy.

At another point in the interview, Ahmadinejad spoke about the differences with America. He said: "the differences between the Iranian nation and the US government are not political or military in nature, but rather they are humanitarian ones. When we say it is to Mr Obama's advantage to withdraw from the Middle East, we are offering friendly advice which we believe is in America's interest."

What does humanitarian differences mean in this context? It is obvious that the honourable president has – once again – spoken on behalf of the people, and attributed the policies of the ruling system in Iran to the people.

This is nothing new. The officials of the Islamic Republic– for years, and whenever it has served their purpose – attributed their views to the people, and acted at their expense. Ahmadinejad has done the same. He cleverly places the Iranian people against the US government, because he considers himself to be the representative of the Iranian nation and believes his policies meet with the people's approval. He doesn't think that, even if we were to accept this impossible assumption, we'd remember that not all Iranians voted for him. The fact is that he does not represent all the people in the country.

It is this erroneous image of representing all Iranians that prompted Ahmadinejad to suggest – after the reporter highlighted the decline of Iran's popularity amongst the other nations in the world – that he, Obama and a European leader should appear in any country in the world together and witness the people's reaction. We must applaud such self-confidence, but as one can see, Ahmadinejad – once more –

considers himself the representative of the Iranian people, and equates his popularity with that of the Iranian people, in other words he regards himself and Iran as being one and the same.

## B) Contradictory words

Responding to a question about the killing of the former Libyan president Muammar Gaddafi, Ahmadinejad said: "We believe that the will of nations should triumph everywhere because justice, freedom and dignity are the right of all nations. The death of an individual or persons is not a cause for joy. We wish everyone to adhere to justice, respect and the rights of all nations."

At another point in his pompous comments, Ahmadinejad spoke on Syria, and said: "The Islamic Republic of Iran has adopted an independent, clear and consistent policy towards all the countries in the world, Iran wishes justice, freedom, respect and national sovereignty for all nations even people in Europe and America. He stressed that the Islamic Republic of Iran condemns violence and killing all over the world, adding that governments and nations can resolve their problems amicably and through dialogue. He said: "NATO or any other party should not interfere in the domestic affairs of countries. We urge all governments and nations to resolve their problems amicably and through mutual respect. Also some countries in the region should not send weapons to this country. European governments should halt their provocative actions and stop applying pressure."

Ahmadinejad's condemnation of the killings stands in stark contrast to the position of the Iranian leaders on the recent events in Syria.

They have openly supported the Syrian government and remained silent on the killing of protestors. Employing his talent for identifying enemies, the leader of the Islamic Republic discovered US footprints in the events in Syria. He has not recognised the movement in Syria as being of the same nature as the movements in Africa. Ali Khamenei has attributed the movements in the Middle East to an "Islamic awakening", even the movement in Syria. Therefore, Ahmadinejad is lying again as he always does. Iran has not only remained silent on the killing of the Syrian people, it has instead given its support to the murderous government of Syria. There is only one obvious reason for this, namely that Syria is Iran's partner in its opposition to Israel. Ahmadinejad remarked: "Iran is trying to mediate in the dispute by starting a dialogue between the protesters and the Syrian government, urging both parties to reach an amicable solution. Reaching an agreement is contingent upon no one interfering in the domestic affairs of Syria." According to Ahmadinejad, no country should meddle in Syrian affairs.

So why is Iran acting in this way? Many countries have highlighted Iran's meddling in Syrian affairs, going so far as to suggest that forces from the Iranian Revolutionary Guard Corps (IRGC) have been dispatched to Syria to crush the opposition.

The CNN interviewer, however, did not touch upon this issue, maybe because we can expect Ahmadinejad to adhere to his policy of denial. What do we expect from Ahmadinejad? He is the same person who looked straight at Christiane Amanpour and claimed that Karubi and Mousavi were not in jail in Iran and were actually free. So, can we actually expect him to admit to Iran's meddling in Syria?

In the interview, Ahmadinejad neither discussed the events following the Iranian elections nor did he mention anything about using a conciliatory approach to reach a peaceful agreement between the authorities and the protesters. The reporter did not ask if the president and the leader adopted this approach when they respectively described his opponents as low-lives and political viruses.

Ahmadinejad described the problems between Iran and the US as one sided – blaming the US. He said: "The problems with the US are one-sided and caused by that government. If the US government truly observed the Al Jazeera Treaty – Article 1 of which clearly states that the US should refrain from actions against Iran – then there wouldn't be any problems today. Unfortunately, the US government has unilaterally violated this treaty." Ahmadinejad, however, didn't mention the takeover of the US embassy following the Islamic Revolution. He didn't say why Iranians acted in such a way and why the officials of the Islamic Republic condoned the action. Ahmadinejad didn't care to explain whether he thought taking over the embassy of a country and calling it a nest of spies was in line with the idea of finding a peaceful and respectable solution to a disagreement.

## C) Propaganda rhetoric and self-grandeur

One of Ahmadinejad's main problems is that he continues to consider himself and his government as a big brother and caretaker of the world. That's why he gives advice to the Libyan government, offers solutions to the problems in Syria and gets involved in Iraq and Afghanistan, and in the process will not spare superpowers such as the US. He offers managerial views to tackling world issues. It would appear that historical differences notwithstanding, one of the major problems that Iran currently experiences with the US stems from the continuing power struggle. The leaders in Iran try very hard to be a major and influential player in the region. Being excluded from the game makes them extremely angry and hostile. This prompts them to resort to retaliatory tactics and a war of words. Ahmadinejad highlights this point in his take on US's tactics in dealing with its opponents. He said: "Instead of capturing and putting pressure on its opponents, the US should listen to them, because Americans have the right to express their views freely. Governments are accountable to their people and must feel responsible for the security and the rights of their people."

The CNN reporter did not ask Ahmadinejad why he had cracked down on the opposition and arrested them. [He could have been asked] *Did you comply with the people's wishes? Did you offer a satisfactory explanation to the people who thought the elections were rigged? If killing is bad then why have so many of your opponents died in the streets and in prison? Why have those charged with levelling insults against you been imprisoned and received lashes? Is the imprisonment of many political figures following the 1388 [2009] elections in line with providing security and being held accountable to the people?*

## D) Shifting the blame

Ahmadinejad said that instead of spending money to maintain its military bases around the world, the US should invest the funds in eradicating poverty and unemployment in its own country.

He said: "The US military budget exceeds one trillion dollars which if it had been spent on that country's economy, events such as the Wall Street crisis could have been avoided." It is astonishing how the rulers in Iran are eager to lend financial assistance to some Palestinian and Lebanese groups, but fail to take one step towards tackling unemployment and poverty in Iran. Ahmadinejad speaks as if Iran is the only country that has entered the internet and cyber news age and that people are oblivious to what is going on in Iran. He effortlessly passes over, with great confidence and self-grandeur, the major and minor problems that concern the people of Iran.

## E) Distorting history and telling lies

Whilst urging Westerners to study history, Ahmadinejad seems to have no interest in the subject himself. During the interview, he commented: "Iran is the only nation that has never been conquered by its enemies." Luckily for him, the interviewer apparently didn't know about Alexander the Great's invasion of Iran, and, therefore, couldn't point that fact out.

I too believe that Westerners should study Iranian history, if for no other reason than to avoid being astonished by such blatant lies.

At another point in the interview, Ahmadinejad claimed that there were no political prisoners in Iran, and that the arrests made following the elections were not prompted by a government complaint. He added that the Judiciary in Iran was independent from the Government and was not influenced by the latter. He insisted that there were times when the Judiciary had opposed the views of the Executive branch.

He pointed out: "There is rule of law in Iran and the Judiciary acts accordingly. Everyone who breaks the law should be held accountable. I'm not happy with the current situation, of course. I don't wish to see anyone put in jail."

Naturally, those who are currently held in the Iranian jails are political prisoners. But obviously there is no clear definition or consensus as to what constitutes a political prisoner in Iran. That's why those who are arrested because of their political activities are not considered to be political prisoners. However, Ahmadinejad apparently has a different reason for claiming that there are no political prisoners in Iran. He maintains that the government has not lodged a complaint against anyone and that the Judiciary had acted independently. So, according to him, an offense is of a political nature only when the government has filed a complaint against a person or persons. Another point worth mentioning is the apparent independence of various branches. Ahmadinejad has repeatedly used this trick to exonerate himself. He said that he was unhappy about the arrests. This tactic, on the one hand, puts a human face on him and, on the other, shifts criticism onto the Judiciary – since it apparently operates independently from the Executive branch.

Ahmadinejad speaks of the rule of law; however, his government has violated the Law more than any other government before it despite the fact that according to the constitution of the Islamic Republic, any group gatherings and marches are permissible as long as they do not contradict Islam.

Responding to a question on the involvement of government officials in banking irregularities in the country, Ahmadinejad said: "Unfortunately, there are some people in the country who have been attributing any incident to my colleagues. I have, so far, not made any decision to either respond or lodge a complaint against them, because I'd very much like for this open climate to continue to exist. I'm certain that these people cannot prove any of their allegations against the government in the courts."

It is obvious that Ahmadinejad doesn't know the difference between an open climate and spreading rumours. To portray himself as an intellectual, he claims to favour an open climate. However, he doesn't mention who was accusing the government so freely, whilst the status quo remains the same. Meanwhile, a student receives lashes for insulting the president. The president attributes this tradition to Western democracy.

However, he fails to mention that in a Western democracy, the press is free and independent and covers any instance of corruption as soon as they discover it. No one escapes their razor-sharp vigilance for finding and disseminating the truth and no government official can shut down a newspaper for printing the truth. The president doesn't clarify his comments for the audience. On the one hand, he complains about the attitude of Western democracy that, he says, attacks his colleagues and, on the other, he expresses his support for free speech. He has apparently forgotten that there is no correlation between Western democracy and Machiavellianism.

# The world community must support the democratic forces in Iran

The history of political developments, in various countries of the world, points to the proven fact that all types of dictatorships have, sooner or later, collapsed or been overthrown by the people.

As tyrannical regimes ignore the will of their people and only rule through repression and crackdowns, they will eventually fall when faced with the revolt of the people against their despotism and they are doomed to be consigned to the dustbin of history.

There is no need to look back to distant centuries in order to prove this inevitable destiny for all dictatorial regimes. We can look at recent and contemporary history and see how the regime in the former Soviet Union, that arose out of a Communist Revolution, fell just after seven decades, despite all its earlier achievements and capabilities as a Superpower, because it denied its own citizens their basic human and democratic rights and cracked down on them when they cried out for freedom.

After the fall of Communism in the former Soviet Union, we witnessed the collapse of its satellite regimes in the East European countries.

Sixteen years after that time, we now witness the fall of the dictatorial regimes in Egypt, Tunisia and Libya. Those countries have now entered a period of transition to democratic systems of government which will undoubtedly soon be followed by other countries that are still under the rule of tyrannical regimes.

The fall of dictators is, indeed, an important chapter in the history of each country that has suffered under their rule, however, as I have mentioned previously, the most important task is how to prepare, in advance, the transition period as it moves towards democracy and to make sure that the regime that follows, will not turn into another dictatorship.

Going through this delicate process of transition to democracy requires different approaches given the social, cultural and political complications of different countries. However, the attention and focus on establishing democratic values and institutions should remain the most important aspect of their progress after overthrowing a dictatorship.

It is only under a democratic system of government that the new governments and their people can bring out the best in each citizen and make a contribution to the progress and development of their country, without having to resort to war or violence.

The history of Western countries indicates that after a thousand year's rule by the Church and centuries of medieval repression, they went through four hundred years of hardship and struggle in order to achieve democracy.

However, the advance of communications and the high speed by which information and ideas travel amongst human societies in today's world means that this process of development and transition from dictatorship to democracy is now much shorter.

Whilst people in East European countries, from Poland to the Czech Republic, could not achieve democracy when the dictators fell, just a decade later they eventually succeeded in establishing democratic systems.

The hope now is that the arrival of democracy in the countries of the Middle East, Libya being the latest of them, will be even quicker than ever before.

Some political and national figures in the countries of the region, especially those in which certain authoritarian tendencies and parties wish to replace dictatorships with their own despotic versions, argue that, as the majority of the people in these countries are Muslims, Islamic traditions are incompatible with democracy and "religious democracies" are the proper alternative for their people.

Sayed Ali Khamenei recently used this term in a speech to attack America and Western countries and claimed that it was "the best form of government for the Islamic world".

However, all these hypocritical and deceiving tactics are only an excuse for the continuation of the religious dictatorship that he and his regime impose upon the people.

It must be said that Democracy is neither a 'Christian phenomenon' nor does it have anything to do with the colour, race or national traditions of any people. It is a clear, alternative system of government compared to all dictatorial regimes.

Another issue here is that given the close and extensive links between the people of the world that we live in today, known as the 'global village', each country can only exist within the framework of its cooperation with the rest of the world, the struggle for democracy in any one country and the attempt by its people to overthrow their dictatorial rulers will not succeed unless it attracts the support of the rest of humanity.

The need for this support becomes even greater during the time of transition from despotism to democracy.

With regards to our beloved country, Iran, as I mentioned in my previous article, the struggle of our people over the course of the last hundred years, since the Constitutional Revolution, shows that in comparison with the other countries in the region, our people deserve and have the unquestionable right to enjoy the fruits of democracy, whilst the Islamic Republic regime has continuously repressed and destroyed all the human and civil rights of the Iranian people since its establishment 32 years ago. Our people have become more resolute in their struggle for the overthrow of this religious dictatorship and they will, following its fall, surely enter a period of transition towards democracy.

Under current circumstances, where the regime has cracked down on all opposition groups, our people need international support for their struggle more than at any time before. Now that some religious groups, within the regime, have turned against it, for their own reasons and interests and are promoting their own version of government, it will not be unrealistic to assume that another type of religious dictatorship will emerge in Iran, should the real democratic forces fail to unite and achieve international support for their objectives.

In trying to justify the lack of support of the US government for the recent freedom movement in Iran, after the 2009 rigged presidential elections, the US Secretary of State Mrs Hillary Clinton recently said in an interview with the Voice of America and the BBC's Persian TV channel that the Obama administration did want to help the movement but that its leaders, inside the country, had sent messages that the US should refrain from doing so.

She then added that if in future the leaders of the freedom movement ask for US support, as the anti-Gaddafi forces did in Libya, America will respond positively.

This is not the right time or place to analyse Mrs Clinton's justifications. However, her statements indicate that the Democrats in the US have not yet reached the conclusion that in order to solve 'the Iran problem', they must separate the Iranian people from the regime, if they wish to see the Iranian people achieve their human rights and stop the regime's sabotaging of the Arab-Israeli peace process and its support for international terrorism. There is only one way of achieving these objectives and that is through the support of the democratic forces of Iran.

Mrs Clinton's claim that Iranians did not want the US government to support their freedom movement in the post-election upheavals contradicts the fact that the same Iranian people were actually shouting 'Obama, you are either with them (the regime) or with us' during their protests. This was the reaction of the Iranian people to President Obama's personal letter to Ali Khamenei but the US government ignored the cries of millions of Iranians for support at that time and, according to Mrs Clinton, only listened to what they heard from two leaders of the movement, Mir Hussein Mussavi and Mehdi Karoubi!!!

This meant that Mr Obama was only interested in listening to messages from two political figures within the regime, whose ultimate aim, in their opposition to the tyrannical regime of the Velayete Faghih, was and still is, to "revive the golden age of Imam Khomeini in Iran"!!!

One must say that it is just as well that the US did not come to the aid of the freedom movement after all.

In conclusion, Iran's pro-democracy movement continues to live despite the regime's wishful claims that it has died away. It will not be long before there is another popular uprising that will sweep the country against the regime, in which most of the Iranian people, with various political and religious tendencies, will take part and when that happens, it will be the moral responsibility of the US, Europe and the international community, in general, to come to the aid of those forces that intend to establish a true democracy in Iran.

# Iran's problems can only be solved by replacing its dictatorial regime with a democratic one

To offer the leadership of a country to a group of people who do not have the right qualifications and knowledge of managing the affairs of that country is like asking a reckless driver who does not even have a licence to drive a bus, full of passengers, through dangerous and mountainous roads.

Naturally, the consequence of using this driver is that all his passengers will perish when he plunges the bus into a ravine.

This is exactly what happened in our own country of Iran. In the aftermath, of a revolution that took place in the name of bringing human rights to the people, the management of the country was given to a group of people who not only did not have any economic or political knowledge, but also were not interested in the prosperity and progress of the country or its people at all.

The only thing that mattered to them was to secure their power with the help of the country's resources and then expand their version of a reactionary, religious and despotic regime throughout the region. From the first day of their rise to power they began their destructive policies that have resulted in nothing but colossal human and material losses for Iran and for Iranians at home and on the international scene.

Against all international laws, the regime's agents occupied the US Embassy in Tehran and held 52 American diplomats and staff hostage for 444 days, which led to three decades of animosity and rift between the two countries and still continues as an obstacle to the normalisation of their relationship.

The diplomatic and economic costs of that act of hostage taking has been immense as the regime was finally forced into releasing the hostages and paying $14 billion in damages to the US government, out of Iranian assets that had been frozen by Washington immediately after the embassy takeover.

For many years after the end of the hostage taking, Iran has been paying hundreds of other fines to US citizens and firms who brought lawsuits against Tehran and by now nothing is left of the billions of dollars of Iranian assets in American banks.

Then, Ayatollah Khomeini miscalculated and thought that he could soon extend his rule over the Iraqi Shias by instigating an uprising against Saddam's regime. Khomeini's plot was a gift to the Iraqi dictator and in view of the bloody purges in Iran's armed forces and the execution of its commanders by the Khomeini regime, he, too, miscalculated that he could now attack Iran and easily capture and annex the southern province of Khuzestan to Iraq.

The two dictators' insanity led to an eight year war between the two countries that resulted in the massacre of hundreds of thousands of people on both sides, millions of maimed soldiers and civilians and tens of billions of dollars of material losses and left the two countries in ruins that have not yet been repaired, not to mention the huge humanitarian and psychological damage that it inflicted on the two nations.

However, Western governments made billions of dollars of profit by arming the two warring countries of Iran and Iraq.

Saddam's miscalculations, however, continued when his army occupied Kuwait. His army was then wiped out by Western armies, whose governments still receive huge compensation and payment from the Kuwaitis for liberating their country. Some years later the US and its allies attacked Iraq itself and overthrew the Saddam regime and are now receiving colossal war compensation from Baghdad for ousting Saddam and brining security to the Iraqis.

Nowadays, the talk of a military attack on Iran has again surfaced in Western media and in political and military circles.

The Islamic Republic regime has refused to stop its uranium-enriching program despite four consecutive UN Security Council Resolutions that explicitly ask Tehran to do so.

Furthermore, Iran has continued with its nuclear programs and has not allowed the IAEA inspectors to visit its suspected nuclear sites and provide the UN Agency with the necessary information that they demand. Last year another concealed nuclear site in Ferdow was exposed by Western intelligence services. The regime had not reported its activities to the IAEA. This has raised the suspicion that the Iranian atomic program has a military objective as the country has barred any visit to its nuclear sites by international inspectors and now has the capability of producing 20 percent enriched uranium, which can be used to make an atomic bomb.

According to the latest IAEA report on Iran's nuclear program, the country has now passed the threshold of having the technology of being able to make an atomic bomb and has already tested the fuel burner for launching such bombs on ballistic missiles.

In IAEA Director General Yukiya Amano's November 2011 report, the Islamic Republic regime of Iran has, for the first time, been explicitly accused of moving in the direction of making an atomic bomb.

The IAEA has unanimously condemned Iran in the report and calls on the regime to provide sufficient, further information about its nuclear activities by March 2012.

The publication of the report has caused grave concern amongst the Israelis who have in the past threatened that they will not tolerate an atomic Iran and will attack and destroy that country's nuclear sites.

It has further been reported that Israeli Prime Minister, Benjamin Netanyahu, and his Defence Minister, Ehud Barak, have the full consent of their cabinet members to launch an attack.

American leaders have, however, opposed the idea and the US Defence Secretary, Leon Panetta, has said that such a military attack will lead to huge and unpredictable consequences in the region.

His French and British counterparts have also warned against the idea and there is little chance of the Israelis attempting to go ahead with this military venture without the support of their Western allies.

Despite all this opposition, one cannot remain certain that such a military attack will never occur as many wars in the past have started when no one expected them to do so. The question therefore remains: What should we do in the event of an Israeli attack on Iran?

We are now witnessing two new developments over the problem of the Iranian regime and its actions. On the one hand, the Saudis have lodged a complaint at the UN about the plot of the Quds Unit of the Revolutionary Guards to assassinate their ambassador in the US and the UN Security Council has issued a resolution condemning the terrorist plot. At the same time, the UN Human Rights Commission is preparing another damning report on the Islamic Republic's record of unabated abuse of the human rights of the Iranian people.

These diplomatic moves and the international condemnation of the regime increase the possibility of a military confrontation with the Islamic Republic, as newspaper reports indicate that the US army has in recent weeks supplied new military hardware to the United Arab Emirates and Bahrain and has extended its presence in its bases in and around the Persian Gulf States.

Despite American opposition to a military attack on Iran, US leaders have explicitly mentioned that, to stop Iran from acquiring a nuclear bomb, they have kept all their options on the table, including a military offensive.

The danger of a military attack on Iran remains a real possibility. As for the Iranian regime and its leaders, Ayatollah Khamenei has continued with his rhetoric against Israel and the US and has said that in the event of an attack on Iran his regime will respond 'with an iron fist'. Ahmadinejad has gone one step further and has predicted 'the imminent fall of capitalism and liberalism in the US and Western countries and an annihilation of the Jewish State of Israel'.

Iran's Chief of Armed Forces, Brigadier Hassan Firoozabadi, has also claimed that if US forces attack Iran 'both the United States and Israel will be wiped from the surface of Planet Earth'.

In the midst of all the problems that have engulfed the Islamic Republic regime and against a background of growing rifts amongst its various factions and the loss of the regime's legitimacy, in the eyes of the Iranian people, because of its repressive crackdowns, Ali Khamenei is plotting to increase his dictatorial grip on power by cancelling the presidential elections in Iran's system of government and appointing a president through the vote of a rubber stamp parliament.

This system of elections does exist in certain countries and, from a theoretical point of view, is a legitimate process. However, in Iran the members of parliament (Majles) are vetted by the Guardian Council, whose own members are directly selected by the Supreme Leader, Khamenei, which means that at the end of the day any "elected president" will be his choice and puppet and not a true representative of the Iranian people.

Sadly, in view of the current chaotic state of affairs in Iran and the unbearable economic hardships, political crackdowns and social problems that the nation is facing, some of our compatriots are so fed up that they will even welcome a military attack on our country if it ends the parasitic life of this corrupt and dictatorial regime.

To borrow a phrase from the famous Iranian poet, Mehdi Akhavan:
*"There is no hope for a national hero to end this misery*
*Let's hope the invader will do this job for us"*
However, we must make the US and Western powers realise that the practical answer to end 'the Iran problem' is not through a war or a military attack. In the event of an attack on Iran's nuclear sites, the regime's nuclear program may be halted and Israel and the West may feel satisfied that they have removed a nuclear threat posed by the

Iranian regime but this regime's threats to world peace and against the Iranian people are not confined to its nuclear program.

As the history of the last 32 years shows, there are three major threats from this regime against Iranians and the Free World, they are the regime's open financial and military support for terrorist groups such as Hizbullah, Hamas and Islamic Jihad, who are involved in activities that threaten stability and peace in Lebanon, Iraq, Palestine and other Arab countries in the region; the regime's opposition to any peace deal between the Arabs and the Israelis and plotting against any peace plans between them, as the events and developments of the last few years in Lebanon, Syria and Gaza have shown. Not to mention, the regime's adversarial policies towards the United States and, other Western as well Arab countries, as shown in the plot to assassinate the Saudi ambassador to US; and last, but by no means the least, and, what really matters most to the Iranian people, is the continuous repression of Iranians and the blatant abuse of their basic human rights by arresting, jailing and executing Iranian freedom fighters and dissidents from every section of Iranian Society.

Solving the threat of Iran's nuclear ambitions will not solve these real and present threats posed by the regime and it is quite feasible that in the aftermath of an attack on its nuclear sites, the regime will actually increase its destructive threats against the international community.

Therefore, the fact of the matter is that the only way to end the "Iran problem" forever is to support the Iranians in their struggle to change this dictatorial regime and replace it with a democratic government.

# Gaddafi's fate awaits all the dictators

B ased on the course of events in Libya, about three months ago, in another article of mine in the weekly Kayhan of London, I predicted that, without a shadow of doubt, the Libyan dictator would finally be found in an underground hole just as had happened to the Iraqi dictator Saddam Hussein and would be punished for his crimes.

My prediction actually came true even earlier than I had expected and the man who called his opponents "rats" and who had sucked the blood of the Libyan people and plundered their national wealth for 42 years was himself finally caught like a running rat and killed on the spot.

With his death one of the longest reigns of a tyrannical and dictatorial regime and its rule of fear and repression came to an end, leaving behind a tormented nation and a ruined country.

This is the inevitable and certain fate of all dictators in the world, whether in Latin America, Eastern Europe, Africa, or indeed the Middle East.

The documented history of the developments of the twentieth century, and the last ten years of the current one, point to the fact that there is no escape, from this destiny, for any dictator.

If it was the turn of Milosevic and Saddam yesterday, and Gaddafi today, then tomorrow it will be the turn of Bashir Assad and many others to fall and face the same fate.

However, this bitter and utterly deplorable trend has sadly continued in backward and undemocratic countries whose regimes have denied their people democracy, the rule of law and freedom.

At the end of each dictator's inevitable fall, the deprived people of those countries paid a heavy price  for having tolerated many years of repression, prison, torture and were finally left with a devastated country, as the terrible legacy of their bloodthirsty rulers who did nothing but plunder the wealth of their country and keep its people backwards and poor.

So, what is the main reason for this deadly and seemingly never-ending cycle of events in backward countries?

The naïve excuse that 'the advanced Western countries are behind the creation of these dictators and their regimes in order to plunder the oil and wealth of those countries' is simply nothing more than a myth.

It is true that foreign powers will always look after their own interests and will even resort to plots and conspiracies to secure them, but the fact of the matter remains that if these plundered countries also had the 'wealth of democracy and the rule of law" and if their people had enjoyed freedom and regarded their governments as their true representatives and could change them through free and fair elections, then foreigners would never have achieved their aims in those countries.

The main problem in backward countries is that they may have huge natural and human resources but they do not have any democracy.

Let's imagine, for a moment, that Libya had enjoyed democracy and had not been under the rule of a dictatorship for 42 continuous years. Then why would there be any reason for so much bloodshed and killing amongst its people just to bring down a tyrant? If they had been ruled by a leader whom they had elected themselves then the people could have ejected him from office after four years and replaced him with someone else who would have responded to their demands. The same would have happened in Iraq, Afghanistan, Tunisia, Egypt, Yemen and Syria, without so many people getting killed and hundreds of thousands getting injured and then ending up with a ruined country.

During the last 70 to 80 years that the Middle Eastern, African and Asian countries have been the scenes of bloody coups, wars and uprisings, neither America nor any European country has had any such event on their soil. This is because these countries are governed on democratic principles and their rulers, whether they are prime ministers or presidents, are democratically elected by the people. When they are replaced through elections, not one drop of blood is shed and no personal hatred or sense of revenge prevails between the losers and the winners of the elections.

In democracies, there is no need for wars, revolutions or bloodshed in order to change the leadership of those countries that are run in this civilised manner, which is based on respect for the voice and votes of their citizens.

The power structure of these countries operates in a way that will not allow any single individual to run for more than two terms and will never have the means of turning himself or herself into a dictator or a lifetime ruler. These leaders are only allowed to exert power within the limit of the law and the moment they try to ignore or cross that limit, the civil and democratic institutions that monitor their actions and deeds will make them accountable and remove them from power.

Alongside this system of government, there operates a free press that acts as the eyes and ears of the people of the country and reports on any wrong doing or corruption amongst officials, without any fear of being intimidated by the State.

From the point of view of the free press, the people of the country are the ultimate judges on the actions of their rulers and politicians.

We all know how this undeniable freedom allowed two American journalists to expose the Watergate scandal in 1970s America, which led to the impeachment of President Richard Nixon.

Only very recently, British Defence Minister, Liam Fox was forced to resign and apologise to the public when the Press revealed that one of his close friends had been involved in abusing his ministerial office for financial gain.

It is so obvious that if a country is run by a democratic system of government, then the energy and effort spent on political conflicts and in-fights over who has more power to abuse it for his own self-interest will be replaced by the united objective of all the citizens for the progress and the development of the country, as the example of the European countries and America shows us.

On that basis, whilst the fall of Gaddafi's dictatorship and others like him in the region are welcomed as opening a new chapter in the history of the Middle East, the most important task now is to make sure that they will walk the right path towards the future by democratising their system of government in order to avoid the return of any future tyrant in their countries.

The management of this sensitive and crucial process of transition towards Democracy will ensure that all the sacrifices that the people have made, will have not been in vain.

We have all witnessed that the fall of a dictator is not necessarily followed by the rise of a democratic system. Eight years after the fall of Saddam Hussein, the political groups and politicians in Iraq have done their best to achieve this objective and so far they have only managed to establish a very elementary form of democracy in the country. During these years a number of outside countries have created some obstacles on the way to this objective by attempting to derail the democratic movements and replace them with a religious regime.

Tunisia and Libya have now entered this transition period and the National Transition Council in Tripoli has the backing of the US, Britain and France as they move towards establishing a truly democratic system.

As far as our beloved country, Iran, is concerned, there is no doubt that after Libya and Syria it will be Iran's turn, to enter this path towards democracy. However, I must add here that the Iranian people, just like other nations, will only require the moral and political (not military) support of Western countries in order to achieve democracy and overthrow the present dictatorial regime.

As someone who deeply believes in the power of democracy, I have established the Council for a Democratic Iran. I am of the belief that the Iranian people are a wise and experienced nation and certainly deserve to enjoy the fruits of freedom and democracy, very much like the people of Western countries and they will certainly attain this noble cause.

Without a shadow of doubt, in a not too distant future, the nightmare of the present religious dictatorship will disappear from our country and our people will enter the crucial transition period towards democracy.

Despite all the repression and crackdowns of the last thirty years, the Iranian people have practised democracy amongst themselves by setting up political parties and groups, launching a free and independent press and campaigning for human and civil rights. However, I believe that we must still equip ourselves with even more practical plans and educational programs to accomplish our transitional period in a successful way. This requires a united and coordinated approach from all of us, which I shall address in my next article.

An international consensus for the removal of the Iranian regime is gaining ground

The isolation of the ruling regime in Iran, on the international scene, has gained unprecedented scope following the passing of three new resolutions by three major world bodies against it, over the last two weeks.

Firstly, the U.N. General Assembly overwhelmingly condemned the Iranian regime for an alleged plot by the Quds Brigade of the Revolutionary Guards to assassinate Adel al-Jubeir, Saudi Arabia's ambassador to Washington.

Secondly, 32 members of the UN nuclear watchdog, the IEAE, unanimously condemned the regime for its failure to cooperate with the Agency and provide it with full details of its nuclear programme and set a deadline of end of March 2012 for it to do so. Thirdly, yet another resolution by the U.N. General Assembly condemned the Iranian regime for its widespread and continuous abuse of the human rights of the Iranian people.

There have been many U.N. resolutions in the past that have condemned the Islamic Republic for its defiance of international law and treaties. However, the passing of three unanimous resolutions by the world's major organisations in such a short period of time is simply unprecedented and can only be interpreted as an international consensus and determination to end what has now become globally known as "the Iran problem".

Only a few days after these resolutions, the British Government took an extraordinary decision and announced that it has imposed sanctions on Iran's Central Bank and severed all their links with Iranian banks and financial centres.

A day after the announcement by the British Government, the United States followed the UK and officially imposed sanctions on Iran's Central Bank and passed a new law prohibiting national and international companies from investing in Iran's oil, gas and petrochemical industries.

The members of the European Union were also expected to announce their own punitive measures against Iran when their foreign ministers met in the first week of December in Brussels.

We had previously foreseen, that in view of the current developments in the Middle East region that soon after the resolution of the Syrian crisis, world attention would, inevitably, turn towards solving "the Iran problem".

The days of the Syrian regime are numbered following the emergence of its deep rifts with the member countries of the Arab League as well as with Turkey and it appears that despite the opposition from Russia and China, who are only concerned with securing their own interests in Iran, the international community has now decisively embarked upon a policy of tackling the pariah regime that is called the Islamic Republic of Iran.

We need to bear in mind that the problem posed by this regime, against the countries of the region and international security, is not just confined to its attempts at making a nuclear bomb. This regime has been particularly causing problems for the international community and its neighbours in three other distinct areas.

For years it has been openly supplying logistical, operational, financial and training support to the terrorist groups of the Middle East and, today, the scope of its involvement in international terrorism has reached Latin American countries. We can see the regime's links with the terrorist groups of Latin America in the plot to assassinate the Saudi ambassador in the US.

The history of the regime's support for international terrorism began immediately after its establishment 32 years ago, with the hostage-taking crisis at the US embassy in Tehran as well as the bombing of the American and French military bases in Beirut and at Al Khobar in Saudi Arabia.

Another major problem that this regime has been causing is its opposition and acts of sabotage against any peace agreement between the Israelis and the Palestinians, despite the overwhelming support of the Palestinian and Arab nations for a just and lasting peace between the two parties.

The Iranian regime has resorted to every conceivable plot at making sure that peace will not prevail between the Israelis and the Palestinians and lastly, but by no means the least, is the issue of the human rights of the Iranian people that have been continuously and blatantly abused by this repressive and dictatorial regime.

The Islamic Republic's support for international terrorism, its opposition to the peace process in the Middle East and its bloody crackdowns on the civil and human rights of the Iranian people were carried out when the regime did not have access to a nuclear bomb. Even if we assume that the current sanctions and international pressures will finally result in the regime abandoning its nuclear ambitions and dismantling its nuclear facilities, it will never, ever stop its acts of terrorism, disruption of the peace process and the repression of the Iranian people. That is why we are now witnessing, along with the imposition of economic and financial sanctions on the regime to stop its nuclear programme, two other resolutions relating to the issues of international terrorism and human rights.

On this basis, this all-inclusive approach of the international community at solving "the Iran problem" can become a prelude for the liberation of Iran from the claws of this brutal regime and the establishment of a democratic and free country.

In other words, the issue of solving "the Iran problem" is in fact a plan for a regime change in Iran.

However, the fact also remains that in the present complicated and inter-related world that we live in, the changing of a regime that has no hesitation in jailing, torturing and murdering its opponents without the slightest concern about the consequences of its actions and justifying them as "religious obligations", is that despite all the sacrifices made by Iranian freedom fighters and democratic forces, regime change cannot succeed without the moral support of the international community. If we want to remain realistic in our fight to change this murderous and repressive regime then we must have the backing of the international community in order to help all patriotic Iranians who are struggling, inside and outside the country, to bring it down.

Needless to say that, despite the claims that the apologists of the regime make in their poisonous propaganda, the support that we are calling for is certainly not to ask the Israelis or the Americans to launch an attack on our Motherland and to liberate our people. That is not true.

No Iranian patriot will ever advocate or accept this scenario. There are many good reasons for rejecting this alternative that I will address in other articles.

What we are calling for is that, the least, the international community and, particularly Western countries, can do for us is to cut off any financial support or link with this barbaric regime and help isolate it even more and leave the task of liberating Iran to the capable hands of the brave Iranian people themselves.

It appears that after three decades of dithering, the international community has now embarked upon this policy of supporting the Iranian people in their struggle to uproot the foundations of this corrupt and murderous regime by imposing paralysing sanctions against it.

In the same way as a dentist will pull out a decayed and dead tooth in order to alleviate the pain of his patient, we must now surgically remove the decayed 'tooth' of the Islamic Republic from the 'mouth' of the Iranian nation. To do so we need Western governments to support the aspirations of our people to a free and democratic country so that they can determine the type of government for themselves, by the power of the ballot box, through fair and free elections.

At the same time the majority of Iranian freedom fighters and patriots recognise the fact that the overthrow of the regime cannot be carried out by a single group or organisation. Those who think the opposite are utopians and we will have nothing to do with them.

The huge task of overthrowing the regime and then establishing a democratic Iran can only be realised thought a united opposition front in which every Iranian, regardless of his, or her, political tendency or social status works to achieve these objectives.

The democratic process by which we seek to create this united front can become the foundation of a future democratic system for the country in which the sovereignty of Iran and its national borders, the separation of Religion and State, the acceptance of the International Declaration on Human Rights, and the holding of a referendum on the preferred system of government for the country, will be the basis of our unity.

In the Council for a Democratic Iran, we work hard to do our share of creating this united front and solidarity amongst our people and following the publication of the reports and articles about our activities and objectives in the weekly Kayhan of London and on the Council's website, some of our fellow Iranians donated various amounts to a total of $1,270,000 to the Council in order to help us with our cause.

Whilst for obvious reasons we cannot name them, we, hereby, sincerely thank them for their generous help and act of patriotism.

# Iranians' struggle for democracy enters an historic phase

World history of the last hundred years points to the undeniable fact that any major change in the destiny of any nation has only come about after its interaction with other countries as we have moved closer to living in what is now known as the Global Village.

In trying to establish a democratic system of government in their country, only people who have wisely interacted with existing democratic countries and learnt from their experiences, have managed to succeed in achieving this notable objective for themselves. Otherwise, any other change in the power structure of their country has simply ended up in replacing one form of dictatorship with another.

In our struggle for democracy, it is of paramount importance that we have a sound understanding of the times and conditions that we live in. In view of the developments of the last few years, particularly in the last few months, it appears that the time for a major and decisive change in Iran has finally arrived, as the Iranian people's objective of changing the repressive Islamic Republic regime is now also shared by the international community.

The Iranian people's opposition to the Islamic Republic regime began immediately after its establishment, when the regime embarked on a brutal suppression and purge of the groups that opposed Ayatollah Khomeini's dictatorial "Islamic government". In the years that followed, this opposition grew larger and became more widespread amongst the various sections of Iranian society as the regime's savage and indiscriminate oppression of them increased.

The serial killing of Iranian writers and intellectuals and the bloody crackdown of the student uprising in 1987 and the massacre and repression of the post-election protestors in 2009 have finally led the Iranian people to seek the overthrow of a regime that has lost all the political or popular legitimacy that it may once have had.

Therefore, as far as the Iranian people are concerned, their position in respect of the ruthless and repressive regime of the Velayate Faghih (Islamic government) is crystal clear. As for those apologists of the regime and the groups that still wishfully think that they can reform this outdated and reactionary system and so keep their "glorious revolution" alive and consequently continue with their failed policies, the tortured bodies of our freedom fighters inside the prisons of their "beloved regime" and the cries of freedom from millions of our suppressed people should awaken them from their dreams and make them realise just how out of touch they are with the aspirations of our people.

These apologists of the regime have no problem with the reactionary system of the Islamic government and its so-called constitution and their "reformist policies" are nothing more than securing the political power of the country for their cronies who played a major role in landing the country in the disastrous condition that it is now in.

Some of these former officials and individuals who have been accomplices in the regime's repression of our people for the last twenty five years have sought refuge in the safety of Western countries and are now wearing the mask of "opposition" with the sole mission of plotting to cause rifts amongst the true opposition groups to the Islamic regime.

However, in the eyes of the Iranian people these bogus opposition elements lack any credibility and are rejected by them and the international community will not count on them too.

As for the international community, despite the overwhelming demand of the Iranian people, the American and European governments have been so obsessed with the regime's attempts to acquire a nuclear bomb that they have imposed economic and diplomatic sanctions against the Islamic Republic with the aim of bringing the regime back to the negotiating table and stopping its atomic program.

Needless to say, that all attempts in this respect have been futile and their policies have actually led to the strengthening of the regime, whose very existence is the main reason for the impasse on the issue. In other words, the international community has concentrated its efforts on getting the regime to reform, instead of changing it and is now admitting that this policy has completely failed.

However, in admitting this failure, Western governments have realised that as long as this brutal and outlaw regime is in power in Iran, then the problems that it has been causing for the security of the world and the region remain and they have now embarked on a policy of regime change in Iran.

The problems posed by this regime to the countries of the region and international security have not just been confined to its attempts to make a nuclear bomb. This regime has been causing problems for the international community and its neighbours since its establishment 33 years ago.

For years it has been supplying logistical, financial and training support to terrorist groups in Middle Eastern countries. We can see the regime's opposition to the Arab-Israeli peace accords and its links with the terrorist groups of Latin America in the case of the plot to assassinate the Saudi ambassador to the US.

The history of the regime's support for international terrorism can also be seen in the hostage-taking crisis at the US embassy in Tehran, the suicide bombing of the American and French military bases in Beirut and the Al Khobar base in Saudi Arabia and its military involvement in Iraq.

It is in response to this catalogue of terrorist acts and its defiance of all international norms and procedures and the non-stop abuse of the human rights of the Iranian people that ,in recent weeks, the UN

Security Council and its atomic agency the IAEA and the UN Human Rights Council have unanimously passed resolutions condemning this brutal and outlaw regime.

On the basis of these resolutions, new economic sanctions on Iranian military leaders and the firms involved in the regime's nuclear program have come into force. Only a few days after these resolutions, the British Government took an extraordinary decision and announced that it had imposed sanctions on Iran's Central Bank and severed all their links with Iranian banks and financial centres.

A day after the announcement by the British Government, the United States followed the UK and officially imposed sanctions on Iran's Central Bank and passed a new law that prohibits national and international companies from investing in Iran's oil, gas and petrochemical industries.

In the meantime, the regime-orchestrated storming of the British embassy in Tehran in which Basiji thugs took the terrified staff hostage for hours and ransacked the Embassy offices and burnt its furniture and files adds yet another act of terrorism and savagery to its criminal record, making Western governments more resolute in their pursuit of regime change to end "the Iran problem" for once and for all.

This means that after 33 long years of bearing its dictatorial and ruthless policies, the Iranian people and the international community are now united in the aim of removing this barbaric regime from power and this presents a historic opportunity for both sides.

There can be no doubt that, for Western governments, the objective of stopping the regime from acquiring a nuclear bomb, comes before the issue of achieving democracy and human rights for the Iranian people.

This makes the task of establishing a democratic country, after the overthrow of the Islamic Republic regime, even more difficult for Iranians who have been the main victims of this regime for 33 long years. We must bear in mind that if our struggle does not bring about a truly democratic system of government to our country then we will just see one dictatorship replaced by another.

Our people are politically mature enough and have gained very many valuable experiences in their long struggle for democracy and freedom and certainly do deserve them. However, to achieve these noble objectives, we must all unite around certain shared principles in order to prepare ourselves for the transitional period for the establishment of democracy in Iran.

# Decayed from inside and under pressure from outside
## Iran's clerical regime faces
## an inevitable collapse

*"**F**ormer presidents such as Rafsanjani and Khatami, who for many years acted as the "moderate" faces of the regime have all been thrown out of the regime's power base."*

The mounting international pressure on the Islamic Republic of Iran and its unprecedented isolation on the world stage have laid the grounds for its inevitable collapse and many Iran analysts believe that the process of the regime's disintegration has already started.

There is no doubt about the paralysing effects of sanctions and the international diplomatic pressure on the regime, however, they are now expected to lead to a fundamental change in the country as they are coupled with an unprecedented level of corruption and decadence that have engulfed the regime since its inception 32 years ago.

Following the US and Britain's imposition of sanctions on Iran's Central Bank, the 27 members of the EU have now decided to do the same as well as putting an embargo on oil imports from Iran.

In the meantime, following the savage attack on the British embassy compound in Tehran by a gang of pro-government Basiji militias which has led to the suspension of diplomatic relations between Iran and the UK, other European countries who do not feel their embassy staff are safe in Iran, have decided to reduce the size of their delegations to a minimum number.

The Dutch foreign minister has even spoken about the possibility of all EU ambassadors being withdrawn from Iran.

Other international organisations including the International Atomic Energy Agency, the UN Security Council, Amnesty International and the UN Human Rights Council have all issued statements in recent weeks, condemning the Islamic Republic regime for its defiance of all international conventions and the abuse of the human rights of the Iranian people.

The sanctions on Iran's financial system will undoubtedly paralyse the   regime's economy whereas the embargo on Iran's oil exports will disrupt the flow of millions of dollars of the nation's wealth that reaches the pockets of the leaders of terrorist groups like Hamas, Islamic Jihad and Hizbullah in Palestine, Syria and Lebanon.

They will also reduce the regime's financial power to employ thugs and mercenaries within the Revolutionary Guards, the Basijis, the judges and security personnel that shut down the voices of dissent and will also hamper its efforts to turn the country into one large prison ruled by armed gangs.

All these factors will contribute to the regime's eventual downfall, but it is the overall social and economic chaos that exists in the country that will  finally bring it down.

The truth of the matter is that if the regime was not so divided and decayed from within then it might still be able to survive external pressure.

No matter how much pressure the international community could put onto a country, as long as there is a feeling of solidarity between the government and the people then not even a war or foreign invasion would be able to change the regime.

It is worth remembering that the Communist regimes collapsed under international pressure only when they had already lost their legitimacy at home.

If external pressures on the regime have only become more serious in the  past few years, the Islamic Republic has been under the pressure of the Iranian people and their protests for many years and has only survived by executing its opponents or jailing and torturing them in a brutal crackdown against any opposition to its policies.

Now, the continuation of the people's struggle and their dissatisfaction have led to rifts amongst the top leadership to the extent that the formerly "united leaders" of the regime are at each other's throats and Khamenei is purging even his closest allies in order to secure his own position in that tyrannical regime.

Former presidents such as Hashemi Rafsanjani and Mohammad Khatami, who for many years acted as the "moderate" faces of the regime, and the so-called reformist camps that supported their policies, have all been thrown out of the regime's power base and not only they do not support Khamenei's camp, they openly oppose the regime's policies and predict the downfall of the whole system if it continues with its crackdown of dissidents at home and its policy of isolating itself from the international community.

So much so that conservative and reactionary ayatollahs, like Janati and Mesbah, accuse the reformists of being "traitors and US stooges who aim to dissolve the Islamic regime and topple it".

In the power struggle that began between the reformists and the Ahamdinejad camp during the Khatami era, Khamenei eventually sided with the latter when he put all his eggs in the basket of the radical president.

However, this policy has not affected his own position as the infighting between the regime's factions, in response to the current crisis in the country, has pitted Ahmadinejad's camp against the Supreme Leader's policies.

Although Ahmadinejad's camp have done their best to discredit many of the founders of the Islamic Revolution, who have fallen out with Khamenei's leadership, the president's camp have, nevertheless, refused to be seen as Khamenei's stooges.

In the case of Iran's Minister of Intelligence, Haydar Moslehi, who was dismissed by Ahmadinejad, Khamenei stepped in and reinstated him against the wishes of the president who did not turn up in his office for two weeks as a protest.

In response to Ahmadinejad's "disobedience", Khamenei's camp began to dig up dirt on the president's close allies and have arrested many of them on corruption charges.

Ahmadinejad's right hand man, Rahim Mashaie, has publicly been branded a renegade who intends to wipe out the clergy from Iran's political scene, whilst his media advisor, Ali Akbar Javanfekr, has been sentenced to one year in prison and disqualified from holding any official position for three years, for publishing an article criticising the Islamic hejab.

Mehdi Tayeb, a close associate of Khamenei and the commander of the Basji's Amar Yasser military camp has even publicly said that the Ahmadinejad camp wants to overthrow the clerical regime.

All in all, the true picture of the regime is one that is fast falling apart from within, having lost many of its traditional power bases amongst the religious establishment and the reformist camps, and is faced with unprecedented economic and political pressure from the international community over its nuclear and regional policies.

When one adds the overwhelming opposition of the Iranian people to a regime that has lost all its legitimacy in their eyes, then the future can only herald a total collapse for a bankrupt and illegal regime in Iran.

# The shining path of democracy will prevail over the darkness of dictatorship

*"Thanks to the many decades of the tyrannical rule of the Jong-il clan, the North Korean people are amongst the least informed people of the world as knowledge and progress go hand in hand with the rule of democracy."*

The two countries of North Korea and the Czech Republic have been mourning the deaths of their leaders in recent days.

Both Kim Jong-il and Vaclav Havel lived their lives under communist regimes, but the former remained loyal to the ideology to the last day of his life, whereas the latter abandoned it in favour of freedom. Jong-il pretended that communism and its doctrines had been "suitable and beneficial" to his people and used it to cling to absolute power.

In contrast, Havel allowed his people to decide freely whether communism was "suitable and beneficial" to them and they rejected it.

Havel never called himself "the shining sun" as Jong-il did, because he did not need it as his people have found the bright path to freedom under him whilst Jong-il was nothing more than a burnt out candle in the dark life of his people.

Havel encouraged his people to question their leaders and hold them accountable to what they say and do, but Jong-il discouraged the North Koreans from ever asking any questions because the regime he led has not been based on the freedom of the individual or basic human rights.

As with all other dictators in history, Jong-il regarded public information and awareness "harmful" to his rule. For many years after its foundation, North Korea called itself a "democratic republic", a deceptive description of a regime that still operates on the principles of slavery where the population are expected to obey blindly the reactionary and tyrannical rule of a single leader who tells them what to wear, what to eat, when to laugh and when to cry.

It has been on the basis of this dictatorial rule that  North Korean leaders have armed the country with an arsenal of atomic bombs because they are always in fear of losing their power, either at the hands of their own suppressed and impoverished people, or those of the international community.

Thanks to the many decades of the tyrannical rule of the Jong-il clan, the North Korean people are amongst the least informed people of the world as knowledge and progress go hand in hand with the rule of democracy.

Under their dictatorial regime, the North Korean people have been placed in an isolated island amongst the nations of the world, where children at the age of three have to be handed over to state institutes so that they can be brainwashed for two years before being returned to their parents. This deeply ideological regime asks for complete obedience from its people who are indoctrinated throughout their life with state propaganda that makes them believe that they owe their existence to the compassion of their "great leader".

In contrast, the people of the Czech Republic decided to build the foundations of their civilisation and democracy on the rubble of communist rule and by doing so, joined the modern world.

Havel knew very well that once his people had tasted the benefits of democracy and freedom they would never abandon these valuable human virtues and would safeguard them from the bottom of their hearts. He never feared a return to the old regime and once he had concluded that his own mission to lead his people to the path of democracy had ended, he voluntarily left his position as their leader.

By then the people of the Czech Republic had gained enough awareness and knowledge about the merits of democracy and how it could offer them a better life and future in a changing world.

In Havel's opinion, the masses were not a total sum of many "minors" who must be led by an absolute leader who determined what was good or bad for his people, as was the case with Jong-il.

Havel proved that the humanism that communism claims to represent is nothing more than a myth, which, in reality, is the exploitation of the masses by a group of privileged and hypocritical people.

For Havel, humanity is equal to the freedom of the individual from the control of the State where democracy, tolerance and the rule of law determined the interactions amongst the citizens, rather than the "wisdom of the great leaders".

The progress of the people of the Czech Republic in the fields of economics, culture, social and health care and their rightful place amongst the nations of the world have vindicated his views, whereas the North Korean leadership remains isolated in the international community, with their people suffering from an inhumane ideology that cloaks itself with the name of humanity.

# Iran's reformist camp boycotts Majles elections as the regime's downfall looms

*"The problem with the Iranian reformists is that they have always tried to derive a democratic interpretation from a system of government that is inherently dictatorial."*

As we had predicted earlier, the ever-increasing rifts amongst the regime's factions caused by the internal socio-political crisis, as well as the international community's economic pressure over Iran's nuclear program have led to a process of disintegration that will eventually bring about the regime's downfall.

This process has now been accelerated by the Front for Reformist Groups' announcement that none of its individual members or organisations will take part as candidates in the forthcoming Majles parliamentary elections, as they consider the contest to be "flawed, staged and lacking in legitimacy under the present atmosphere of crackdowns, with so many political prisoners behind bars".

The announcement is certainly a devastating blow to the regime and will undoubtedly lead to further rifts within the remaining factions.

Whilst some conservative factions may rub their hands with glee that the absence of the reformists may make their undisputed position even stronger, their "wiser" elements, as well the Supreme Leader, Khamenei, know very well that this development heralds more bad news for the future of the regime.

At the time of Mohammad Khatami's presidency, Ali Khamenei

once said that "the survival of the Islamic Republic system depends on the conservatives and reformists acting as the two wings of a bird, and if one of them goes missing then the bird will certainly fall".

However, the reformists have been the target of intense crackdowns and purges within the regime over the last three years with many of their leaders jailed and all their political groups and parties banned.

As early as nine months ago their surviving figures set a number of conditions to the regime for their participation  in the Majles "elections", including the release of their leaders and equal and free access to national TV and radio stations, none of which have been granted.

In fact, the demands led to further crackdowns and pro-Khamenei clerics like Ahmad Khatami and Ahmad Jannati have dismissed them as "the plea of a bunch of guilty and greedy individuals for forgiveness so that they could repeat their crimes".

The reformist front  has also said that they will not support any other candidate but have stopped short of boycotting the Majles elections as a safeguard in order not to be accused of "collaborating with foreign powers", a charge  commonly used by the regime against anyone who opposes it.

Analysts say that the statement is an indirect admission by the reformists' camp that they have failed to reform this regime and that the new composition of its leadership lacks any legitimacy.

The reformists have arrived at this conclusion after having been in power themselves for many years whilst the Iranian people paid a heavy price through the martyrdom of hundreds of their youths and the imprisonment and torture of thousands of others at the hands of this tyrannical regime.

However, for Iranian freedom fighters and impartial analysts of Iranian affairs, this reality had long become clear and the fact that the reformists are now confessing to it reflects their own dilemma of not being able to justify their vacillating stance to the public any more.

The problem with Iranian reformists is that they have always tried to derive a democratic interpretation from a system of government that is inherently dictatorial.

Although this regime carries the title of a "republic", which in its classic description must mean a democratic system of people ruling over themselves, the suffix of "Islamic" negates its republican feature as in the traditional Islamic government of many centuries ago, God is considered as the actual ruler of the country.

The system becomes even more dictatorial when the notion of Velayate Faghih, or the absolute rule of the clergy, wants us to believe that a single individual, Khamenei, must decide the destiny of a nation, as he is "God's representative on earth".

The experience of the past 30 years of this Islamic government in Iran only indicates that no matter who is chosen by the people as their presidential or parliamentarian representatives, at the end of the day, they are nothing other than a stooge of the Valiye Faghih, who is above the Law and the heads of the three organs of the State must obey his orders.

No other system of government in the modern world is as dictatorial and tyrannical as that of today's Iran and the reformists have been seeking to establish "Islamic democracy" through this medieval and despotic system for decades!

However, now that they have finally concluded that their policies have been misleading the nation and have decided to change course. This will certainly lead to wider implications as the majority of the Iranian people, who until the last presidential elections in 2009, had hoped that they could still find prosperity and freedom through the ballot box, have now realised that the only way to achieve these objectives is to overthrow the Islamic Republic.

# Iran's impoverished ethnic minorities: united despite the regime's systematic suppression

*"If the Arabs of Iran who live in the oil-rich southern province of Khuzestan compare their living conditions with the high standard of life that Arabs in neighbouring countries enjoy then they will have every right to feel neglected by the Islamic Republic regime and the miseries that it has brought them."*

In the long and mostly turbulent history of Iran, its ethnic minorities have always borne the brunt of keeping the country united.

At times they have been supportive of the central government, whilst there have been other instances when they have risen up against them. Occasionally, they have given the ruling regimes the excuse to deny them their rights and suppress them with ease.

Whilst these tensions have historically existed in the distant past, it could be argued that the worst cases of these confrontations have come to the fore since Iran's 1905 Constitutional Revolution.

During the rule of the Pahlavi Dynasty of Reza and Mohammad Reza, Iran's ethnic minorities had a relatively peaceful relationship with the central government ruling from Tehran even though they still had many legitimate grievances, but since the Islamic Revolution of 1979 this relationship has turned into one of full scale political and military confrontation as, in contravention of its own Constitution, the Islamic regime has followed a policy of racial and religious discrimination against them.

According to Article 19 of Iran's Islamic Constitution, "the Iranian people, from each and every ethnic minority and regardless of their race, religion, colour, language or any other cultural identity are equal citizens of the country and no ethnic group has any privilege above another".

However, in practice, the rulers of Iran have systematically ignored the principles of this Article, as with many other Articles of their own Constitution, and have added to the previous inequalities, so that the oil and gas-rich province of Khuzestan is now amongst the most deprived areas of Iran.

A glance at the position and status of the same ethnic minorities in the neighbouring countries that border Iran indicates how patient and modest have been Iran's ethnic minorities and, at the same time, how their tolerance and endurance of the hardships that they have suffered has actually led to even greater abuses of their rights by the regime.

If the Arabs of Iran who live in the oil-rich southern province of Khuzestan compare their living conditions with the high standard of life that Arabs in neighbouring countries enjoy then they will have every right to feel neglected by the Islamic Republic regime and the miseries that it has brought them.

They have the same source of revenue, in the oil and gas of the province they live in, as do Arabs in neighbouring states and if they were to demand independence for themselves, they would become as prosperous as the other rich countries in the region.

The province of Khuzestan has offered its vast oil and gas reserves to the rest of the people of Iran because the people of Khuzestan look upon themselves as being part of the nation of Iran and bear the difficulties and hardships that the nation suffers as a result of the mismanagement of the country by a regime that, in return, does not pay any attention to their needs.

The post Iran-Iraq war destruction in this southern Iranian province can still be seen everywhere some 20 years after the end of that devastating conflict.

If the Kurds of Iran were to compare their own status to the Kurds of Iraq then they would have every legitimate right to feel how they have been denied their basic human and economic rights by the regime that rules from Tehran.

The same goes with the Azeri and Turkmen people of Iran, once they look at themselves and realise how far behind they are compared to their ethnic brethren in the neighbouring countries of Azerbaijan and Turkmenistan.

However, despite all the inequality and economic discrimination against them, the decent and honourable ethnic minorities of Iran have, at the turning points of the history of our country, remained loyal and paid a heavy price to protect the sovereignty of our Motherland and have never used the repression of the central government as an excuse to sell out to invaders.

How could anyone forget the sacrifices that the Arabs of our country made during the war against the Iraqi invaders?

Our Azeri minorities were at the forefront of fighting for democracy and justice during the Constitutional Revolution and without the heroic leadership of Sattar Khan and Baqer Khan that Revolution would never have succeeded.

According to documentary evidence, the Azeris of Iran had the largest number of our nation's martyrs in defending our motherland during the war with Iraq. They have made immense economic and artistic contributions to the social and cultural fabric of our country.

Our Kurds, Baluchis and Turkmen who belong to the Sunni sect of Islam have never remained indifferent towards defending our national interests, even though the Islamic Republic regime has continuously fanned the flames of religious sectarianism since its establishment, so much so that, to this day, our Sunni Muslims do not even have their own mosque in Tehran, which the regime claims is "the capital city of the Islamic world".

Despite living mainly on the borders of Iran, our ethnic minorities have never contemplated breaking away from Iran and have paid a heavy price for their loyalty.

On the contrary, the Islamic Republic regime has always taken advantage of their sense of patriotism by looking upon our noble ethnic minorities as if they were responsible for safeguarding the borders and should not expect any favours from the central government in return. When drawing up the country's economic plans, the regime allocates a tiny budget towards the deprived areas of Iran that have a high population of our ethnic minorities.

Whilst economic and political injustice is commonplace all over Iran, they are far greater against the ethnic minorities of the country. In some remote parts of Iran, our ethnic minority communities are even denied the most basic social, educational and healthcare services, which is indicative of the presence of undemocratic government in Iran and is fraught with corruption and mismanagement.

It should, therefore, not come as a surprise if our toiling ethnic minorities rise up against this injustice when they are classified as second class citizens by a regime whose tyrannical rule is the root cause of their deprivations.

In my opinion, the emergence of armed and terrorist groups amongst these minorities, like the Rigis in Baluchestan, are the direct result of the regime's blind bigotry and discrimination against the Sunni minorities.

A regime that sows the seeds of religious and ethnic hatred can only expect to reap the wrath of those whom it oppresses and which leaves them with no other option but to take up arms against the State.

The discrimination against our ethnic minorities is not only confined to social and economic issues. If language is the main aspect of an ethnic minority's identity, then we can safely say that the regime's refusal to allow our minorities to use their own ethnic languages in the educational system is the worst possible injustice that a government can inflict against its own people.

All the children of our ethnic minorities are forced to learn the national Farsi language before they are even able to speak in their own ethnic language.

This is not to say that the Persian language does not play a major role in the overall unity of our people nor to deny its richness and literary value, but the promotion of the ethnic languages of Iran will in fact enrich Persian as many of our ethnic languages derive from it.

Sadly, the question of supporting our ethnic languages has always been smeared with the accusation of advocating the partition of our Motherland.

Our ethnic languages have survived many thousands of years and indeed have lived in harmony and peace with Persian, as our national language, in what appears to have been a very democratic coexistence that has benefited everyone.

The many inscribed tablets that have been excavated in our ancient cities appear in the various ethnic minority languages of the land of Iran and no one regards them as "an attempt to partition Iran" in our past history.

In fact, they are testimony to the history of our people's sense of tolerance and peaceful coexistence amongst the many different people that make up our nation. In other words, the ethnic minority languages act as a means of connecting us together rather than dividing us.

This means that unless the citizens of a country have a sense of belonging to a particular geographical and historical entity, they will never have unity amongst themselves and democracy will never flourish amongst them.

The ethnic minorities of our beloved Iran are an inseparable part of our long history and proud culture and identity. We must all demonstrate our commitment to acknowledging the multi-ethnic composition of our country in order to be able to achieve our united objective of acquiring democracy for Iran.

The day when all Iranians, regardless of their ethnic, religious, ideological and gender differences live in a free and democratic country and benefit equally from the resources of this ancient land under one flag is not that far away.

The Iran of the future belongs to all of us!

# Iranian women as prime victims of the Islamic Republic's violence and injustice

*"The seemingly trivial issue of the hejab cover for women has been at the centre of three decades of heated public debates and social strife in Iran, with the government constantly using it to crackdown on women's rights activists."*

The leaders of the Islamic Republic regime have never believed in social and political freedom for women and have constantly created many barriers for their presence in the public life of the nation.

The only "benefits" that Iranian women have received from the Islamic Revolution have been forced domestitude, the obligatory hejab, removal from many public office jobs, a revival of polygamy and becoming second class citizens in their own country.

Despite providing more educational and work opportunities for women, the view of the leaders of the Islamic Republic regime about women is that they should remain as mothers or housewives.

This traditional perception of women runs in contrast to the regime's pretence that it stands for "women's freedoms".

Principally, the policy makers of the regime prefer women to stay at home and look after the affairs of the family, rather than join society. This cultural attitude stems from the fact that the Islamic leaders of Iran look upon women as being sexually able to tempt men with their "satanic attractions", which corrupts the foundations of families and society.

This is exactly the sexist view that looks upon women as sex objects, the very accusation that the Islamic Republic's leaders have been directing against Western culture for decades to justify their own restrictive policies on women.

It is in line with this reactionary and sexist attitude that Iranian universities and their courses are segregated between male and female students, government offices have male and female departments that deal separately with men and women, women are banned from going to sport stadiums, public transport is divided between men or women-only seats along with a plethora of other backward discriminatory practices.

What the regime is not interested to hear is the cry of Iranian women against this discrimination.

The "jewel in the crown" of the regime's reactionary acts of injustice against Iranian women is its obligatory hejab cover that came into force on the first day of its coming to power. Nearly 80 years before then, led by the progressive and revolutionary Tahereh Ghuratolein, Iranian women had resisted that degrading cover and refused to accept it as a symbol of their surrender to the then male dominated society of Iran.

To force the women of a society to wear a hejab cover as part of their clothing amounts to taking away the basic human rights of an individual to decide what they wish to wear, an issue that in modern and democratic societies is the least of problems for its citizens and governments.

However, this seemingly trivial issue has been at the centre of three decades of heated public debate and social strife in Iran, with the government constantly using it to crackdown on women's rights activists and impose its repressive policies towards those who oppose the hejab.

In today's modern and democratic countries, it is an accepted social norm that an individual's choice of what to wear, or, what not to wear, is entirely a personal matter but when this issue becomes the preoccupation of a government, then it can only show how reactionary and despotic the system of government is in that particular country.

In the case of Iran, it must be noted that before the Islamic Republic regime came to power in 1979, Iranian women, whether Muslim or non-Muslim, were free, either to wear a hejab, or not to, and this issue never presented itself as a social problem. It is noteworthy that the great majority of the hundreds of thousands of Iranian women who live in Iranian communities outside the country never wear the hejab.

The Iranian regime has never asked Iranian women, inside the country, whether they wish to wear the hejab or not, as in line with its dictatorial rule, it has decided, on their behalf, that they must wear it and must not oppose it either.

For many years the Islamic Republic regime criticised Western culture for its "sexist view of women" that looks upon them as "sex objects".

However, the most progressive laws in support of women's rights and their protection against domestic violence, sexual discrimination or sexist policies are in place in the Western world, none of which can be seen in the Islamic Republic, where women are defenceless and are treated as second class citizens in their own country.

Although Iranian women have shown their capabilities in achieving higher education, the regime's employment law have always barred them from entering the job market on an equal footing with men. In fact, a recent government policy is driving many female civil servants to leave their public posts and work from home on a part-time basis, where they also have to look after the affairs of their families, which puts further hardship and responsibilities on their shoulders, whilst at the same time denying many of their human rights.

Despite all these discriminatory and repressive policies, brave Iranian women have always been behind many of Iran's social movements in the last century. The names of women like Tahereh Ghuratolein, Zaynab Pasha, Bibi Maryam Bakhtiari have been inscribed in the history of Iran's Constitutional Revolution of 1905, as heroic leaders in our people's long struggle for freedom and democracy.

No one can forget the immense sacrifices that our sisters and mothers made during the unwanted war with Iraq in the 1980s even though the rulers of our country returned their contribution and vital service to the front with further repressive actions after that conflict.

History will never forget the crimes of the Islamic Republic regime against our women, great numbers of whom have become the victims of the regime's firing squads, jailed, tortured, raped and repressed for opposing its anti-female policies.

The younger generation of Iran may not know that women became the regime's first victims after it came to power. Thousands of young and old women met their deaths at the hands of the regime in the political purges of the early 1980s in Iran.

Not many people perhaps have heard of the name of Farokhro Parsa, the female Minister of Education during the time of Mohammad Reza Shah Pahlavi, who was killed by the insane judge Khalkhali in the most heinous way just because she had served under the old regime.

But we have  certainly all heard the names of Neda Agha Sulatna, Taraneh Mousavi, Haleh Sahabi, Hoda Saber, Shabnam Madadi and many more members of the young and forward looking generation of Iran and how they were murdered, tortured to death or imprisoned by the regime when they demanded their human rights.

The sadistic and barbaric torturers of the regime have brought on themselves an eternal curse by raping, torturing and harassing thousands of our women over the many years that this tyrannical regime has been in power in our country.

The younger generation of Iran has heard the name of heroic women like Nasrin Sotoodeh whose only "crime" that causes her to be in a solitary cell, has been her profession of acting as an independent lawyer for political prisoners.

Our young generation have seen with their own eyes how a young woman by the name of Samiyeh Tohidlou was flogged by the executioners of this tyrannical regime on the bogus charges of "insulting the President".

Today, Iranian women of all ages are at the forefront of our people's struggle for democracy and human rights and act as the most powerful opponents of the regime.

The martyrs of the current democracy movement in Iran, such as Sohrab Arabi, are the children of many brave mothers who have brought them up in a spirit of fighting for their human rights. To bring up such freedom fighters in a closed society ruled by tyrants is an impossible task that the brave women of Iran have managed to achieve, despite all the odds against them.

It is upon this reality that I can see a day when all the citizens of a free Iran, women or men, Muslim or non-Muslim, religious or non-believer, will live alongside each other in peace and prosperity, where no one will be condemned to injustice on the grounds of gender, race, colour or beliefs.

On that day, which is not too far away, Iranian women will be equal citizens of our nation and our men will learn to respect them.

# Young people are the backbone of Iran's democracy movement

*"By the time young Iranians finish their education and face the many social, cultural and economic barriers that the regime has created on their way to realising their potential, they lose much of their enthusiasm and become mentally aged people who are more a burden to society than useful members of it."*

In his studies of  Iranian mythology, Arthur Christensen, the renowned Danish orientalist, reminds us of the story of Zahak, a despot whose life and tyrannical rule depended on feeding the two snakes on his shoulders with the brains and blood of two young Iranians every single day.

There is no doubt that the young generation of every country secure the continuation of their society and are amongst the most active and creative sections of their communities.

Under authoritarian regimes these young and forward-looking social forces are the targets of the worst repression, as dictatorial regimes are the worst enemies of freethinking and creativity, the two main characteristics that young people possess.

The present Zahak-like rulers of Iran treat the young people of Iran with contempt because they ask very many legitimate questions that the reactionary and backward regime is unwilling and unable to answer, they want to stifle them so that they cannot even have the desire or power to raise those questions in the first place.

To be able to question or criticise one's rulers, one must live in a democratic society where the voices of dissent can be aired freely without fear of persecution, those conditions do not exist in today's Iran. The tyrannical regime of Iran is not interested in listening to these voices and deals with them by cracking down on young writers, journalists and students. The regime not only represses young people's aspirations and hopes, it also tries to brain wash them to stop them from even contemplating any dissent by limiting their access to the free world, changing the contents of their textbooks with reactionary material, discriminating against student activists and purging their secular and progressive teachers and lecturers from the country's educational system.

Iran has a unique large young population. The very definition of being young equals to a desire of an individual to be enquiring, experimenting, aiming for high education, looking for decent jobs, being in love and looking for a partner for life, marrying and finding a home to live with one's spouse and children.

However, the insanity of the regime and its devastating policies have deliberately diverted the attention of young Iranian people from these natural human instincts by keeping them preoccupied with trivial matters whilst interfering in every aspect of their individual and private life.

During the post-election protests of 2009, young Iranians clearly demonstrated their strong opposition to the regime's dictatorial rules and became the subject of its worst crimes. Hundreds of them were gunned down on the streets by the Basij armed militias and the security forces, thousands of them were sent to prisons and squalid dungeons where many of them were tortured to death and raped, as the story of their mistreatment was reported in the world's media at that time.

The crackdown on Iranian youth since then has continued as the regime has realised the potential of this major force for any political change in Iran.

The regime may have provided better access to higher education for young Iranians in order to keep them busy with their studies, but once the educated elite leave university, they then have to join an army of jobless and deprived young people, whilst the regime busily channels hundreds of millions of dollars of the nation's wealth to extremist groups in the Middle East.

By the time young Iranians finish their education and face the many social, cultural and economic barriers that the regime has created on their way to realising their potential, they lose much of their enthusiasm and become mentally aged people who are more a burden to society than useful members of it.

The irony is that in today's Iran, a bunch of power thirsty geriatrics plan and decide the life of millions of young Iranians who are the future of the country. Even when the regime pretends that it is interested in the wellbeing of young Iranians, it will only invest in a number of undeserved supporters of the regime who are handpicked for their loyalty to its bankrupt ideology and policies.

The problem of unemployment and, consequently, not being able to get married and support a family has forced many young Iranians into depression and dependency on drugs.

The plundering of the wealth of the country by the regime's mafia-type factions or spending its wealth in foreign countries to buy support for the regime has left young Iranians with no source of social benefit care, they either resort to drugs in desperation, or try to flee the country in order to survive their unbearable conditions. Concern for the welfare and future of our youth are at the bottom of the regime's list of priorities.

Those of them who manage to reach the safe shores of foreign countries will flourish and show their true potential, in contrast to being constantly repressed and humiliated by their rulers in Iran. Democratic countries offer them every opportunity to realise their potential and become useful members of their communities.

They no longer have to listen to the tormenting orders of a reactionary and repressive regime as to what they are allowed to wear, what hair style they must have, why they should not walk hand in hand with their boyfriend or girlfriend in public and that if they disobey these orders they will end up in jail for "acting against the security of the state and having been deceived by foreign intelligence services".

The ultimate aim of the regime is to demoralise and turn young Iranians into automatons who will never question its inhumane ideology and repressive policies.

This makes the young generation of Iran the largest potential opposition force to the current rulers of Iran, they need to receive the attention of all those dissident groups and individuals who are struggling to bring democracy to Iran.

The young people of Iran are sick and tired of all types of authoritarian rulers and as the rightful owners of the Iran of tomorrow, they demand respect, attention and understanding of their social, political and educational needs. At the same time, they are mature enough to shun extremism and adventurism, as they are aware that in today's world, democratic principles and dialogue amongst nations are the norm.

Those who in the name of our young students savagely attack foreign embassies and take hostages have nothing to do with the Iranian people's long traditions of promoting peace and justice and are nothing more than a bunch of thugs and stooges of a regime that has taken the whole nation of Iran as its hostage.

In line with its manifesto, the Council for a Democratic Iran fully supports the struggle of Iranian youth for freedom and human rights, in addition to the Council's unwavering support for the rights of women, students, artists, and journalists in Iran.

The Council firmly believes that the dark days of our country will soon come to an end through the united struggle of all the Iranian people for democracy and human rights and that the young generation of Iran will inherit a liberated and prosperous country for themselves and their own children.

# The Statement of Council for Democratic Iran
# In support of the struggle of
# the Syrian People

It is now one year since the start of the uprising of the Syrian people, which bears all the hallmarks of their aspiration to achieve democracy for their country.

Undoubtedly, the will of the people of any nation is the main factor in establishing democracy and all tyrannical regimes will resist their just demands and aspirations in this respect and in the process resort to massacring their own people.

The Assad regime has not been an exception and over the last year has launched a bloody crackdown on the Syrian people's democratic movement.

As with all other dictatorial regimes before it, the Assad regime will one day hear the voice of the Syrian people, but that day will be too late.

It is crystal clear that what is happening in Syria today is a blatant abuse of the human rights of the people by a regime bent on resorting to crimes against humanity, just to stay in power.

The Council for a Democratic Iran, in line with the Iranian people, the victims of very similar atrocities perpetrated by the Islamic Republic regime in Iran, strongly condemn the participation of the Iranian regime's criminal agents in the crackdown against the Syrian people.

It is not a coincidence that the tyrannical rulers of Iran have come to the support of Assad's dictatorial regime as they know very well that the liberation of the Syrian people from their despotic regime, will send the waves of freedom from Damascus to Tehran.

The Council for a Democratic Iran therefore states its full and unconditional support for the heroic people of Syria in their fight for democracy as part of its own struggle for liberating Iran from its despotic rulers.

We sincerely hope that our moral and humanitarian support for the Syrian people will go some way to alleviating the deep and bloody wounds that the Assad regime has wrought upon them and we hope that the shining sun of democracy will finally brighten up their destiny in a free and democratic Syria, in the same way as it will eventually happen in Iran.

On that day the people of our two countries will start a new era of friendship blessed with liberty and prosperity for our two ancient nations.

**The Council for a Democratic Iran**
**March 2012**

# The many different but united groups for the freedom of Iran

*"The Iranian people have tactically retreated form the streets in their battle against this barbaric regime and cleverly moved into the trenches of the cyber highways, which has now opened up a new front for their struggle."*

On the surface it may appear as though the freedom movement of the Iranian people has fizzled out and that, as the Iranian regime claims, it has finally managed to stifle their struggle for liberty and justice, which it refers to as "subversion".

However, a glance at the realities of Iranian society will prove otherwise. If the 2008 post-election mass protests were based on an emotional reaction to the rigging of the votes of the citizens by the ruling regime, then the "silence and calm" that followed their presence on the streets should not be regarded as the end of their protests or, for that matter, the death of the movement.

It goes without saying that by "emotional reaction" I do not mean that the Iranian people did not have any reasonable and realistic demands during their mass demonstrations at that time. As a matter of fact, they did and they demanded to know what had happened to their votes, which meant that they were quite aware that the elections had been rigged.

Appearing on the streets in their millions and asking the authorities to give them back their rights and to respect their electoral choice was nothing more than an emotional act, which was the main reason for the failure of the movement at the time.

However, the bloody crackdown of the people's peaceful protest revealed to them that they are facing a ruthless and savage regime that only uses religion as a cover for its barbaric policies and keeps the nation in chains and the people as its slaves.

It was only too natural, that faced with the regime's savage crackdown, people had to retreat from the streets as the alternative would have been to die at the hands of the butchers of a system that was, and is, prepared to resort to jailing, torturing and killing people with no hesitation, just to stay in power.

But if the Iranian people tactically retreated form the streets in their battle against this barbaric regime, they cleverly moved into the trenches of the cyber highways, which has now opened up a new front for their struggle against the ruling regime.

I do not consider this change of tactics in taking our struggle into the social networks as a wrong move, especially when the regime's leaders are rightfully harassed by this 21st century magical means of communications and do their best to disrupt it by any means they can.

However, using social networks and cyber highways in our struggle can only be justified so long as it does not mislead our youth into substituting it for reality and solely relying on their application to pursue their aims. This will, in the long run, neutralise young people in pursuing their objectives.

There is no doubt that using social networks for mobilising our forces against this barbaric regime will lead to fewer numbers of casualties amongst our freedom fighters. In fact, using social networks can even deceive the regime by making them wishfully think that they have put an end to our struggle and that we have vanished. By thinking so, the regime may decide to use less show of force in public.

Another advantage of using the Internet and social networks in our struggle is that it provides us with ample time to rethink our next moves and tactics. The open and generous world of the Internet freely allows everyone to take part in exchanging their views with others, without the fear of persecution.

In other words, social networks provide a perfect ground for us to practise democracy. Let's not forget how the Internet, Facebook and Twitter played such a crucial role during the Arab Spring.

Social networks also act as a preliminary forum for finding and recruiting likeminded compatriots for victory in our struggle against the regime, an issue that has sadly been absent from amongst Iranian opposition groups for too long.

To draw a comparison, not even two members of a sports team may think the same, but they are all equally united in their pursuit of winning the match against their opponents.

Therefore, the presence of many different points of view in our united struggle against the tyrannical regime is not only a positive thing but it also strengthens our position in confronting its savagery.

Unfortunately, the exiled opposition groups have not been able to sit around a table to listen to each other's views as long as our personal or group interests come before the interests of the people of Iran, then our individual efforts will not make any headway in our struggle, no matter how useful or great they may be. The Islamic Republic regime has invested many years in seeing us disunited so as to be able to crackdown on us with a free hand.

The coming together of different individuals and groups in the Iranian opposition does not mean that they will have to lose their identity or compromise on their objectives. We must never aim for a unity based on turning everyone into one identity. On the contrary, this is against the very principles of democracy, which guarantees the rights of people being different in their opinions and the way they wish to pursue their civilised objectives.

If we were to ask every individual or political group to follow one school of thought then we will end up with the same disastrous consequences that the current Islamic Republic suffers from, i.e. a ruthless dictatorial regime.

The beauty of having a rainbow coalition of various opposition groups united around certain mutual objectives is that each one of us can then present our points of view and objectives to the people of Iran in a democratic process and they will be the ones who will judge whether to accept or reject them.

It is only through this process of coming together that the tree of democracy can be planted in the land of Iran and later blossom with prosperity and happiness for our people in a future free and democratic country.

# Who were the losers in the recent Majles "elections"?

*"The new Majles deputies will all be a minority of pro-regime individuals who have nothing to do with the aspirations of the majority of the Iranian people and are only serving a dictator and his cronies."*

The Majles deputies are all a minority of pro-regime individuals who have nothing to do with the aspirations of the majority of the Iranian people and are only serving a dictator and his cronies.

A review of the structure and practices of the last two of Iran's Majles (parliaments), where the ultra-conservatives have had the upper hand and the Guardian Council purged most of the reformists deputies from even entering the legislative bodies, clearly indicates that this is now nothing more than a rubber stamp institution and a puppet parliament that exist just to sustain the regime in power.

However, the leaders of the Islamic Republic still regard parliamentary elections as an important opportunity to pretend to the world that Iran is a democratic country where people can freely choose their representatives, and at the same time buy legitimacy for themselves on the international scene.

Whilst the number of Iranian people taking part in the Majles elections has traditionally been much lower than those voting in the presidential elections, nevertheless the predicted low turnout combined with the boycott of the forthcoming elections by most Iranians will prove to the World that the people of Iran unanimously reject this regime and its leaders.

I say "to the World" because the regime will do its best through its national broadcasting organisation mouthpieces and dailies like Kayhan and the Fars News Agency to claim deceitfully that the very people whose interests and existence are completely ignored by this tyrannical regime "have turned up in their millions to vote and that the authorities have been forced to extend the voting hours".

The propaganda scenario of lies and deception is the hallmark of this regime and follows every single election event in the country, after which we are told that "the people of Iran have today made history and shown the world how loyal they are to their rulers".

However, the truth of the matter is that today the majority of the Iranian people have completely lost their trust in this regime which forces them to vote only for those who have been vetted and then selected by the Guardian Council once their absolute loyalty to the leaders of the regime has been proven. In other words, only those who obey the orders of the clerical leaders are allowed to run for the Majles, not those who wish to represent their constituencies.

Despite knowing that disqualifying even the most loyal of their opponents from running in the Majles "elections" will lead to apathy amongst the population and deter them from voting, the "elections" are nothing more than stage shows for the regime, as it does not care about the number of votes since, after all, its own puppets will be chosen to enter the Majles.

This, in effect, means that the future Majles deputies will all be a minority of pro-regime individuals who have nothing to do with the aspirations of the majority of the Iranian people and are only serving a dictator and his cronies.

In other words, what really matters to the regime is just to hold the elections for the sake of staging a show. Any election that could provide an opportunity for the opposition forces to voice the aspirations and needs of the Iranian people will be regarded as a major threat by the regime, given the explosive social and political conditions in the country.

An independent and probing Majles whose deputies are not the sheepish followers of the Supreme Leader's orders can be a thorn in the side of the regime. The Supreme Leader has, indeed, shown in the past, on more than one occasion, that when the majority of the deputies have not followed his orders, he has used his "exclusive powers" to overturn their decisions.

However, he has always tried to use his powers behind the scenes in order to avoid being exposed as a dictator whose corrupt regime has no stomach for democracy and is more interested in the affairs of Syria, Palestine and Venezuela rather than Iran.

On the day of these sham elections, the majority of the Iranian people will stay away from the regime's stage show in order to declare their united rejection of this hypocritical system that has no respect for their wishes and aspirations.

The action will be a big NO to the regime and will be a memorable day in the history of the Iranian people's struggle for democracy. By doing so, the only true winners on that day will be the Iranian people.

# Anti-imperialism or anti-democracy?

*"The historical fear of the West and its intentions towards Iran amongst the country's intellectuals and opposition groups stems from a mentality that only sees everything in black or white and has its roots in the Cold War era."*

The Iranian writer Jalal Al-Ahmad's book "Westernisation" a criticism of the modernisation of the Iranian Society in the 1960s was a best seller amongst his contemporary intelligentsia as well as the radical clergy who opposed the Shah's regime for their own reasons.

The book advocated radical anti-Western politics by opposing the "plundering imperialists" but at the same time carried serious contradictory arguments as Al-Ahmad lacked any coherent philosophical credentials.

All he had done was to benefit from the very means that a Western-type democracy had provided him to criticise the West, in the same way as his followers amongst the Iranian clergy did by using the freedoms of the Western media to stage their revolution but once in power they turned against everything that Western democracies had offered.

The Iranian regime's anti-Western policies have even reached the field of human and social sciences by deleting them from the country's educational system as they deal with freedom of thought and secular ideologies, issues that the despotic regime routinely suppresses in today's Iran.

The leaders of the Islamic Republic regime used the same anti-imperialism slogans that were once the exclusive commodity of the former Soviet Union in order to oppose Western countries to the extent that the objective of "overthrowing the imperialist powers" replaced the objective of achieving the democracy that they had promised to the Iranian people in return for participating in a revolution.

In other words, overnight a revolution in the name of freedom had turned into one that demonised the West as a Satan that must be destroyed.

The roots of this fanatical and hysterical animosity with the West amongst the Iranian mullahs could be found in the thinking of people like Al-Ahmad and have, so far, cost the nation of Iran very dearly.

However, whilst it is understandable that the reactionary clerics in Iran may have a natural tendency to oppose Western democracies as they are based on the separation of Religion and State, it is a matter of surprise to see, that even today, some Iranian opposition groups whose members have lived in Western countries for decades, still speak of the West with the same vocabulary that the backward mullahs use. They do not seem to have overcome their old and antiquated ideologies and dogmas and look upon the West as the source of their misfortunes.

Whilst these groups will keep talking about the merits of democracy and their opposition to the tyrannical regime in Iran, their deeds contradict their claims as they can hardly tolerate anyone who opposes their politics. The result of this lack of tolerance and acting in an undemocratic manner means that we now have dozens of Iranian opposition groups inside and outside the country, no two of which can agree on a united platform of action against the despotic regime in Tehran.

The historical fear of the West and its intentions towards Iran amongst the country's intellectuals and opposition groups stems from a mentality that only sees everything in black or white and has its roots in the Cold War era. This mentality could not accommodate itself with Western democracies as its own "credibility" lies in denouncing them.

However, in my view, the examples of South Korea and Japan teach us that countries and people can keep their traditional values and ways of life and still benefit immensely from closer political and economic ties with Western industrial democracies. A quick comparison between the years of North Korean dependency on the former Soviet Union and pro-American South Korea is a good example of this argument.

Japan's post-World War II economic links with the US, which was its most powerful foe at the time of that conflict, shows how a country can progress immensely and become an industrial giant once it does not allow historical animosities to block the prosperity of its people.

Iran's opposition forces need to exercise democratic values if they are serious about bringing democracy to the Iranian people. To build the democratic and prosperous Iran of tomorrow we must cleanse our minds of any historical suspicion of the West, if we are to avoid a repeat of the disastrous Islamic Republic regime for our country. To carry the misleading slogans of the past into our future means that we shall never be able to build a democratic country.

We must in fact learn from Western democracies and how they function on the basis of tolerance and respect for their citizens' human and civil rights and the Law.

The Iran of tomorrow needs those Iranian democrats for whom the interests of the country have priority over personal interests.

Iran's opposition groups must strive to increase their level of tolerance towards one another. This should not mean that all must follow one ideology, which would defeat the objective, but more of learning how to unite around the objective of what is best for Iran and its people whilst we remain loyal to our own points of view. Only then can the dream of a free and prosperous Iran be made real.

# Beyond the Messages from Iran

My latest article in the Persian- language, Kayhan of London, received a widespread response from our people inside Iran, especially from the much-tormented military personnel of our country. Frankly speaking, I had not foreseen such a far-reaching reaction to one newspaper article. Maybe I was still under the wrong impression that as the Iranian armed forces were now part of the repressive organs of the regime and that there was hardly any difference between them and the Revolutionary Guards, therefore nationalist sentiments and patriotism and the love of our motherland have no place in the hearts and minds of our armed forces and that the once powerful Iranian army of yesteryear has now become a tool in the hands of the regime after three decades of ideological brainwashing of its soldiers and commanders alike.

In the Kayhan article I pointed out that the very fabric of our armed forces is intertwined with Iranian nationalism and thirty years of the Islamic regime's attempts to erode this from the minds of our military personnel have been in vain.

The messages that I received from our fellow Iranian people via e-mails, Facebook and direct telephone calls proved two important things to me; that Kayhan speaks for the people of Iran and their aspirations, particularly those of the Armed Forces, and that when one speaks the truth, it is welcomed by the people.

I have been involved in our people's struggle against the Islamic Republic regime for many years now. Even though the regime plundered my family's wealth and forced us into exile, when the tragic Bam earthquake of 2003 happened and thousands of my fellow countrymen and women became homeless, I rushed to their help with whatever means I had in my possession.

It was actually during my trip to Iran for this particular purpose that I realised how much damage and torment the Mullahs had wrought upon my country.

As a consequence of that visit, I pledged to myself and to God to dedicate my life and donate whatever financial means I had, to the holy cause of liberating my beloved Iran from the claws of this regime.

# Fighting for survival through war and destruction, Islamic Republic style

The Islamic Republic's intransigent position in the crisis over Iran's nuclear program and its secret efforts to acquire technology in order to make an atomic bomb as well as the regime's continued support for international terrorism and meddling in the affairs of Iraq, Palestine and Lebanon have now led to its unprecedented isolation amongst the world community that have brought about the recent spate of sanctions against Iran.

Cornered by an ever increasing and paralysing external and internal pressure, the regime has now resorted to warmongering tactics as a way out of its crisis ridden status by increasing its threats against Western countries and their regional allies which will, in turn, give them the excuse to enter a military confrontation with Iran.

The truth is that a faction of the political and military decision makers in the Islamic Republic believe that the only way out of the current crisis, that has engulfed the regime, is a military attack on Iran by either the Israelis or the US forces based in the Persian Gulf countries as it can then inflame Iranian nationalism and use it to silence the dissidents at home and reduce the pressure of the international community on itself by plunging the whole region into a wider conflict.

It does not matter to this regime as to how many thousands of people may perish in such a conflict and what colossal collateral damage it may suffer, so long as the regime survives another day and continues with its destructive policies.

It is interesting to note that whilst the Islamic Republic regime is bent on plunging Iran into a military conflict for its own spiteful objectives, it blames its opponents inside and outside the country for Iran's existing problems. The regime and its various agents are not alone in levelling these ridiculous accusations against dissidents and exiles, as those apologists and groups who have been purged through the regime's infighting and are hypocritically presenting themselves as the "opposition" also shamelessly repeat the same allegations.

These apologists of the regime have infiltrated the television networks and launched dozens of websites with the help of dubious financiers and constantly use the media to attack those who do not subscribe to their version of reformist policies and who call for the overthrow of the regime as "collaborating with the US and Israel to launch a military attack on Iran in order to come to power."

This accusation is directed against all those opposition groups and organisations that call for the overthrow of the regime rather than ally themselves with the groups that wishfully think that they can reform this regime. All those organisations that seek to remove the regime from power have quite clearly stated their fierce opposition to any military attack on Iran as they too are Iranian patriots and are quite aware of the extent of the disastrous consequences that such an attack will have for our fellow Iranians and the future of democracy in our country.

Furthermore, the regime uses this accusation to increase its crackdowns on the pro-democracy activists inside the country and turn it into a full police state.

The main concern, of the real opponents of the religious dictatorship ruling Iran, is how to take our country through this critical stage and lead it towards Democracy and Freedom and at the same time avert any foreign invasion of our Fatherland. They have enough political and diplomatic wisdom not to fall into any traps that are laid by the regime and its apologists.

Contrary to the regime's claims in this respect, its own military and political leaders are edging Iran towards a military confrontation with the Western Powers by meddling in the affairs of the neighbouring countries of Iraq, Afghanistan and the Persian Gulf States and hampering all peace efforts between the Arabs and Israelis by supporting the extremist groups in Lebanon and even explicitly threatening Turkey with a military attack.

Western countries have always stated that they have all options available to them and prefer a diplomatic resolution of Iran's nuclear crisis but the Islamic Republic regime is only interested in talking about a war which shows its hidden desires to make this happen.

Following the sanctions imposed on Iran's Central Bank by the US and British governments and the EU's embargo on Iran's oil exports, some of the high-ranking military personnel in the regime have threatened the West with the blockage of the Straits of Hormuz through which a quarter of the World's oil and gas supplies pass every single day.

The regime has made this threat with the full knowledge that the Western powers will not allow Iran to close the Straits of Hormuz to international maritime traffic, which acts as a lifeline to many industrial countries across the globe.

However, verbal threats were later followed by a two day war game by the Iranian navy in the waters of the Persian Gulf and once that finished the Revolutionary Guards naval units staged their own 10 day long manoeuvres, which were widely reported in the regime's media and satellite channels in order to scare off Western governments and their allies in the region.

The commander of Iran's navy, Habib Abusayari, has said that Iran's armed forces are capable of closing the Straits of Hormuz but in the final analysis most experts believe that the threat is nothing more than rhetoric from a regime that ignores the fact that the Iranian people will never back a tyrannical and barbaric regime. The regime is, therefore, resorting to all possible means to prolong its detestable existence.

# Iranian regime broadens the spectre of war

*"Today the clerics in Iran have turned into a group of Stalinists who have set up a wall of separation between the Iranian people and the rest of the world. "*

A glance at the deeds of the Islamic Republic regime over the last 33 years clearly tells us that it has always injected terror into the lives of the Iranian people by making them fear the regime's crackdowns as well as the anxiety of facing a military attack on their country by foreign powers.

In the eyes of the hysterical rulers of Iran, especially, its supreme leader Ali Khamenei, almost all the people and governments of the world are their enemies and have supposedly disguised themselves as journalists, bloggers, activists and foreign envoys.

It appears that eight years of a bloody war with Iraq, that Ayatollah Khomeini reluctantly agreed to cease by accepting a UN resolution and which he likened to 'drinking a chalice of poison', has not been enough for the leaders of the Islamic Republic to learn from their deadly mistakes and to try and co-exist in peace and harmony with the rest of the world.

All they needed to do was to have a look around the country and realise how much damage their adventurist and irrational policies have done to the economy and the social and political fabric of Iran and then adopt a policy of mutual respect for the neighbours of our country in order to secure the peace and sovereignty of Iran. Sadly, we are dealing with a regime that is an expert at wrecking all the opportunities that could help serve the interests of Iran and the Iranian people and the result of that negligence is in front of our eyes in today's Iran.

Today the clerics in Iran have turned into a group of Stalinists who have set up a wall of separation between the Iranian people and the rest of the world.

This point was very cleverly picked up by US President Barack Obama when in his Norouz message to the Iranian people he said that the rulers of Iran have now drawn an electronic curtain around the country in order to stifle the desire of the Iranian people to be part of the international community.

If during the Cold War, the former Soviet Union's Communist leaders had put an Iron Curtain around their empire in order to cut their people off from any contact with the free world, then today the Islamic Republic regime follows the same tyrannical method by denying the Iranian people free access to the Internet and the flow of information.

In other words, the Iranian regime is a Soviet-type despotic regime that feeds on fanning the flames of animosity between the Iranian people and the outside world, for the sole purpose of keeping itself in power. It should not, therefore, come as a surprise that Tehran has very close links with Moscow as the Iranian rulers look upon the former Soviet dictators as their mentors in their hypocritical anti-Western policies.

However, if the former Soviet Union leaders never allowed the Cold War to turn into a full scale military confrontation with the Western countries, then the Iranian regime has gone one step forward and provocatively antagonises the West by its suspicious nuclear program, thereby, inviting a war whose massive destructive effects will reach far beyond Iran's borders.

However, I believe that if such a war were ever to happen then it will certainly see the end of the present regime in Iran, even though its collapse is already looming  without a military escapade.

I will refer to the Iranian regime's domestic and foreign policies as "talking through the bonnets". The regime treats the historic people of our country with complete contempt for their peaceful nature and characteristics such as a strong desire for fairness and justice. A people whose history carries a clean record of always advocating tolerance amongst the many and various ethnic and religious peoples within its own boundaries and peace with the outside world.

The fact that the great Iranian poet Saadi's call for the unity of Mankind and love for one another is inscribed at the entrance of the United Nation's headquarters is a good example of this claim.

Sadly, the warmongering fanatics of the regime have eviscerated this fact and the danger becomes even greater when we know that, when the regime eventually becomes cornered and desperate, it will betray the Iranian people by offering concessions to foreign governments.

Only last week, after the US government exempted Japan and nine other countries from its oil sanctions against Iran due to a major fall in the level of their dependency on Iranian oil, the head of the Majles Committee for National Security and Forcign Affairs, Alauddin Borojerdi, called it "a humiliating US retreat".

This rhetoric of a senior member of the  governing faction indicates that the rulers of the Islamic Republic regime do not even welcome any change of policy by foreign powers that may help to resolve the nuclear crisis peacefully and are only interested in an antagonistic and adversarial approach to and from the outside world. In other words, they want the Iranian people to live under the constant spectre of confrontation and war, the elements that this tyrannical regime survives on.

# Iran's regime is an accomplice in the genocide of the Syrian people

*"Despite the Iranian regime's open support for Assad's massacre of his people as being justified under the guise of "resistance against Zionist plots", Tehran is privately concerned about the post-Assad era in Syria."*

The crimes of the Islamic Republic regime are not merely confined against the Iranian people. Nowadays, they have extended into taking part in the genocide of the Syrian people at the hands of Assad's tyrannical regime.

In the mind of the despotic rulers of Iran, the freedom movements in the Islamic countries of Bahrain, Libya and Egypt are the effects of the "Islamic awakening" that the Islamic Revolution supposedly brought about, but the same cannot be said about the Syrian people because their rulers are the regional ally of the Tehran regime!

In other words, as far as the Iranian regime is concerned, the only criterion for any freedom movement in any country of the world is that it is in line with its policies. If it is, then it will receive its propaganda and lip service, and if it is not, then it must be crushed by the rulers of that particular country!

In his recent meeting with the Turkish Prime Minster, Recep Tayyip Erdogan, in Tehran, the regime's supreme leader, Ali Khamenei, explicitly said that he, and his whole regime, will oppose any peace plan for the Syrian crisis by the international community if the Western governments and the US play a part in that plan.

This statement goes to show two things. Firstly, the Iranian regime is prepared to see hundreds of innocent Syrian children, men and women, old and young, being butchered by the Assad regime every single day just because the Western governments may be involved in a peace plan for that country. So much for the regime's claim to "Islamic values".

Secondly, one can see the shallowness of this regime's understanding of, how in our modern and complicated world, diplomacy and negotiations can avert conflicts and bloodshed. What else should one expect from the regime when its domestic and international policies are based on repression at home and terrorism abroad?

The leaders of the Islamic Republic claim that their unwavering support for the Syrian regime is because "it is in the first line of resistance against the Zionists" in the wider Arab-Israeli conflict.

Again, here the rulers of Iran are turning a blind eye to the massacre of the Arab and non-Arab Syrians just because the Israelis may be engaged in a similar confrontation with the Palestinians. The Iran regime's hypocritical stance clearly shows that for the rulers of the Islamic Republic we have only two types of human beings in this world. Those who think the same as they do and deserve to be protected at all costs whilst those who think and act differently from them must perish.

Over the years it has become apparent that the "support" of the Iranian regime for the Palestinian people is nothing more than a political stunt and that its policies in respect of the Arab-Israeli peace efforts have always been to derail any peace plan between the two nations, leading to the continuation of a bloody and tragic conflict.

In fact, the many years of the Assad regime acting as Tehran's proxy in the Arab-Israeli conflict in order to hamper all the peace efforts that will deny Tehran its anti-US and Israeli rhetoric, must somehow be "rewarded" by the Iranian regime, hence Tehran's isolated backing for the Syrian dictator against his own people.

However, despite the Iranian regime's open support for Assad's massacre of his people as being justified under the guise of "resistance against Zionist plots", Tehran is privately concerned about the post-Assad era in Syria.

Already several "forward looking" members of the regime have indirectly cautioned Khamenei on the issue and said that Tehran must not put all of its eggs in Assad's basket, given the international condemnation of his ruthless regime and Iran's own isolation amongst its Arab neighbours who have unanimously condemned Assad, not to mention the choking economic sanctions that will soon lead to major social strife within Iran itself.

For a long time, the Iranian regime has used the plight of the Palestinian people in order to justify its antagonistic stance against moderate Arab states but the Syrian tragedy has blown its cover wide open since the people of the Middle East are wondering whether the blood of a Syrian Arab is different from that of a Palestinian Arab. Sadly, as far as the rulers of the Islamic Republic regime are concerned, it is.

# Iran's political elite must come clean about backing religious despots

*"The young generation of Iran must ask their parents why they put their trust in those opposition groups that passed the leadership of the Revolution to a bunch of reactionary and bigoted mullahs who know nothing about politics and statesmanship?"*

History has witnessed many revolutions that, despite their initial slogans in defence of freedom and reform, have later deviated from their objectives and ended up as being more corrupt and despotic than the regimes they replaced. The Islamic Revolution in Iran has not been an exception.

The Islamic Revolution has cost the Iranian people dearly. Despite the Shah's own admission at the time that the country was suffering from a lack of democracy and that "he had heard the voice of the Revolution", it was too late for any gradual reform and his regime and country were swept away by the destructive tides of the Revolution.

With hindsight, if the values of the 1905 Constitution Revolution, achieved by the sacrifices of our ancestors, had been assiduously observed by the former regime, then there would have been no need for another revolution in 1979.

Nowadays, the younger generation of Iran blames their parents for their participation in the Islamic Revolution and asks them why they helped to overthrow the Monarchy and replace it with a religious regime, when that change has resulted in so much pain and misery for the nation?

In my view, this common question in the minds of the young people of Iran does not entirely represent the truth. The youth of Iran need to see the revolution of 1979 in its context. The Iranian people of the early 1970s had many justified demands, which the former regime had overlooked and ignored. When a government denies its own people their rights and aspirations then, sooner or later, protests will burst out into the open.

Add  the monarchy's repressive methods of jailing and suppressing the elites of society and stifling the voices of those dissidents who wished to echo the demands of the people, then we have a full recipe for insurrection and revolution.

Once the voices of moderation and reform were cracked down upon then violence took over from dialogue and this happened in Iran in the years leading to the Islamic Revolution.

The young generation of Iran should consider these facts when they judge their parents for what they did 33 years ago and respect them accordingly.

To live in the past and thinking that it was somehow better than the present is not the rational way of thinking and leads to a feeling of helplessness in changing the conditions that we live in now and stops us from moving towards a better future.

Needless to say, the Iranian people made many errors of judgement in the course of the 1979 Revolution and did not act in time to correct them.

The revolutionary turmoil brought out a great many political groups and parties onto the streets and from the point of view of the unity of the nation in demanding change that was a positive development.

However, the Iranian people made the huge mistake of trusting the political elite's alliance, made up of nationalists like the National Front and the Freedom Movement,  communists like the Tudeh Party and the Fadayian Khalq and radical Islamist groups like the Mujaheddin Khalq and left their fate in those hands once the old regime had been overthrown.

The young generation of Iran must ask their parents why they put their trust in these groups and organisations that passed the leadership of the Revolution to a bunch of reactionary and bigoted mullahs who know nothing about politics and statesmanship?

I have no quarrel with our political elite. The Islamic Republic regime has brutally purged them from every aspect of our country's social and political life and executed thousands of them. However, we must ask why, despite their expertise and high education and many years of struggle for democracy and human rights under the former regime, they so naively left the scene and followed the leadership of the clergy or remained silent when they knew that the outcome of a religious government will be nothing but a tyrannical dictatorship?

In my view, the political elite and the intellectuals of Iran did not act responsibly enough to promote the aspirations of our people for freedom and progress in the 1979 revolution and by accepting the leadership of the Clergy, they in fact betrayed the Iranian people and all those who gave their lives to bring about Democracy in Iran.

The current political elite must compensate for the massive miscalculation of its previous generation. We all know very well that the present tyrannical regime would not have been able to establish its bloody rule over our country, if certain political groups that are now in opposition had not aided it in the early days of the Revolution.

All those opposition groups that are now struggling to free Iran from the claws of this reactionary and despotic regime must first gain the trust of the Iranian people. The Iranian people are not a "silent majority". On the contrary, they are ready to enter a new phase of our struggle for freedom and democracy, once they are certain about who can genuinely lead them in achieving their aspirations.

This puts extra responsibility on the shoulders of our political elite and dissident groups to respond to our people's demands and urgently organise their struggle in one united front against the despotic clerical regime that has driven our Motherland into a situation that threatens the very existence of Iran as a nation State.

Our dissident and opposition groups must avoid regarding themselves as being the "only rightful voice of the Iranian people" as the Iranian people will immediately reject them for their authoritarian and undemocratic stance. The Iranian opposition is not the exclusive club or property of any individual or group and all those who want to bring about a secular democracy and the rule of law and human and civil rights, to the Iranian people, have an equal share in it.

It is high time that the Iranian political elite and opposition groups unite around these principles and on the basis of the bitter experience of the past we shall all build a free, democratic and prosperous Iran in the future, on the ashes of the present regime.

# Failure - the only outcome of the new nuclear talks with Iran

*"The dilemma for the Iranian regime in its nuclear talks with the West is that they have so heavily invested in reaching a position where they can show themselves off as a regional power, but at the same time, they have to relinquish that power in order to survive."*

The November 2011 nuclear talks between the 5+1 countries and Iran that were held in Istanbul ended in a stalemate as Tehran had put forward certain conditions which, if not met, meant that it would not return to the negotiating table. Astonishingly, these conditions had nothing to do with the issue of Iran's suspected nuclear program and were about the regime's concerns about the regional policies of the Westerns powers.

However, the intensification of the economic and trade sanctions together with increasing international diplomatic pressure forced the Iranian regime to drop all their pre-talk conditions and swallow their rhetoric and once again sit round a negotiating table with the 5+1 countries in Istanbul, earlier this month.

If we go by what the regime's leadership and preachers have been saying about these recent talks, then one may think that they will have a positive result at the end, but, all the indications are that this will be wishful thinking.

At the same time as the Istanbul talks were taking place, Commander Javani, the advisor to the Supreme Leader's representative in the

Revolutionary Guards, told the Fars News Agency: "Iran has always shown its goodwill in the nuclear talks and there is no reason why we should now reconsider some aspects of our current nuclear program".

Javani also reiterated that the Islamic Republic "will not budge" to the Western countries' demands.

The analysis of Javani's comments indicates that the Iranian leadership, or at least, a certain powerful and influential faction of them, is not serious about any compromise on Iran's nuclear standing.

Javani's comments should not be mistaken as propaganda rhetoric. They reveal a behind the scene rift amongst the leadership of the regime on where they go from here with their nuclear program.

What does Javani mean when he talks about "certain aspects of Iran's nuclear program"?

He is obviously playing down the significance of the regime's retreat from its long held position in the face of international pressure by suggesting that Iran has shown flexibility and goodwill in its talks but behind this misleading comment lies the regime's fear of collapsing under the unprecedented trade, banking and financial sanctions that are choking Iran's already sick economy, not to mention the threat of a military strike on the country's nuclear installations.

Whilst Javani claims that Iran will should not have to show any more flexibility in its stance towards the West, the main demand of the Western countries still remains the suspension of Iran's uranium enrichment activities and further transparency in its nuclear program that must be certified by the International Atomic Energy Authority's inspectors, who have been denied access to certain nuclear installations in the country in the past.

One must not forget that Javani's comments reflect the position of the very person who put him in his job, that of the Supreme Leader, Ali Khamenei, who has repeatedly said that Iran must never retreat from its position on the nuclear issue as this will give an upper hand to Western governments in any negotiations and put further pressure on his regime over other issues such as human rights and the regime's support for extremist groups.

A review of the Iranian regime's foreign policy since its inception 33 years ago proves that unless they are put under pressure and feel threatened, they will always continue to defy international norms, with absolutely no concern for the national interests of Iran and the Iranian people In this respect, the Iranian regime is an identical twin of the North Korean regime, with the difference being that the North Koreans will go all the way to defy the international community with their nuclear threats, but the Iranian regime will quickly move to defuse any existential threats by retreating under pressure.

Tehran's show of strength by staging several military manoeuvres and testing long range missiles, in recent weeks, have even caused concern in Moscow, which has long supported its nuclear program.

The dilemma for the Iranian regime in its nuclear talks with the West is that they have so heavily invested in reaching a position where they can show themselves off as a regional power, but at the same time, they have to relinquish that power in order to survive.

Western governments have already rejected Iran's demand to begin lifting some of the economic sanctions before next month's talks in Baghdad, throwing the possibility of the talks taking place in question.

The Iranian leadership's intention by raising this demand is to make the West look like the party that was not seriously interested in a peaceful resolution of the nuclear crisis and, thereby, continues with its secret programs.

This policy of playing games with international public opinion is also followed by Western governments, except that they have a far greater influence in convincing the international community that Iran was not sincere in its approach, thus paving the way for dealing with the crisis in an alternative manner.

Whatever the outcome of this new round of negotiations, the Iranian regime is a loser in this game. Either, it will perish in the crisis that it itself has created, or it will collapse, from within, for not being able to handle the consequences of its adventurist policies.

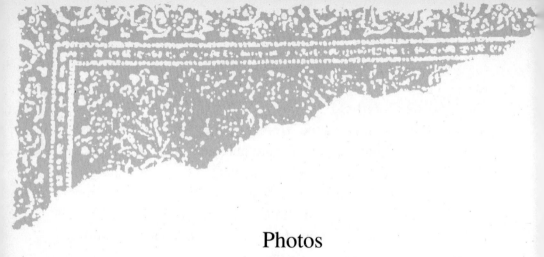

Photos

Behrooz Behbudi in 1959 in Tehran, Iran

Behrooz and father Abbas Behbudi in 1950, Manzarieh Gardens, Northern Tehran

With my son Abbas (Noah) in West Vancouver, BC , 1997

Father, Abbas Behbudi in 1974 in Tehran at family's winter home

My daughter Forough (Elizabeth)

My father, mother and sisters in Tehran, 1964

The Behbudi family gathering at our summer home in Abe Ali, Iran, 1967

L to R: Cousin Syrous Farahmand, father Abbas Behbudi and Behrooz in 1964, Tehran, Iran

Grandpa Ghanbar Khan at the Shah's villa in Abe Ali in 1967

Family gathering in Tehran, Iran, 1965. L to R back row: Elfi Behbudi, uncle Hossieni Fallah; second cousin Lt. General Farahmand; aunt from father's side, Tallat Behbudi; mother, Forough Behbudi; uncle Mehdi Behbudi. Children in front L to R: Cousin Faranak; sister Nazzy; cousin Bahman Sameni-Fallah; cousin Thomas Ghovanloo

L to R: Sister Nazzy Behbudi, Cousin Syrous Farahmad, seated in middle is second cousin Mansoureh Farahmad-Behbudi, Behrooz Behbudi and cousin Faranak Farahmad

With my sister Nazzy on holiday by the Caspian Sea in 1959

With my father at our summer house in Abe Ali, Iran

Graduating from University of British Columbia in 1974, Vancouver, BC, Canada

Meeting with the Shah at his summer palace in 1972,
as the leader of students studying abroad.

Meeting with his Holiness, Pope John Paul II in 1998, the Vatican, Rome

Speaking at the US Senate in 2010

Presenting US Senator Sam Brownback with
the "Award of Defenders of Democracy"
at the US Senate in Washington, DC, 2010

With Hon. Bijan Kian, one of the main speakers at the Defenders of Democracy event in the US Senate in Washington, DC, 2010

At a reception in the US Senate

Dr. Behrooz Behbudi, Founder of CDI presenting the Award of Defenders of Democracy 2010 to the representative of the US Congress

Visiting the Capitol Hill, Washington, DC 2010

*To Behrooz*
*Best Wishes,*

With the former President Bush and partner Dr. Sonny Lee

To Behrooz — With appreciation and all best wishes, Elizabeth Dole

L to R: Senator Elizabeth Dole, Dr. Behrooz Behbudi, Senator Robert Dole, 2008

At the National Arts Club in New York in 2005, meeting with Foreign Minister of Turkey and currently the President of Turkey, Abdullah Gul

L to R:  Dr. Alden James Jr., President National Arts Club of New York, Dr. Behrooz Behbudi and John James, 2005

Dr. Behrooz Behbudi, Senator Al Damato in New York at Senator Damato's office in 2003

With Prince Ali Seraj of Afghanistan in Greenwich Connecticut at the CDI function to raise awareness about Afghanistan in 2005

With Queen Noor at a New York reception

With the late fashion designer Bijan and sister Nazzy in Washington, DC, 2008

L to R: Mr. T Davar-Panah, Dr. Behbudi, President Asif Ali of Pakistan, the late Prime Minister Benazir Bhutto and Gesina Thompson (Dr. Bohbudi's Architect), attending a wedding reception in Dubai

With the Canadian ambassador and his wife in Canada's Embassy in Tehran

With Reverend Dr. Bill Bright, at the Campus Crusade for Christ meeting,
New York, 1997

Business meeting with the Ambassador of Qatar to South and North America
in 2000 in the Qataris' New York Embassy

Special Prosecutor Kenneth Starr (in the case of President Clinton and Monica Lewinsky) with Dr. Behrooz Behbudi in Washington DC in 2006

With Senator Elizabeth Dole in Washington DC at the meeting of the National Republican Senatorial Committee in 2006

L to R: Uncle Dr. Karim Rokhnejad, Dr. Behrooz Behbudi, Deputy Minister of Health, Mr. Khatami (the brother of President Khatami) and members of the Global Unity Partnership team to discuss charitable matters between the Global Unity Partnership and various ministries in Iran in 1998

On a Mission in Virginia to discuss charitable projects in Iran in 2000

With Sargent Shriver, Chairman of the Special Olympics, Washington DC

Special Olympics sponsors' meeting in Washington, DC in 2008

**Upcoming Events**

**July 2002**
Nelson Mandela's Children's Fund 84th Birthday Celebration

**Summer/Fall 2002**
Nadia Comaneci and Bart Conner Special Olympics Tour of Romania

**September 2002**
Special Olympics China National Games and Regional Youth Summit
– Xian, China
Special Olympics Middle East/North Africa Regional Games and
Regional Youth Summit – Ba àlbak, Lebanon

*William Friel; Magda Moussa, President of Special Olympics
Egypt; Timothy Shriver; Ismail Osman; Her Excellency
Suzanne Mubarak, First Lady of Egypt*

*i am sam stars Joseph Rosenberg, Michelle Pfeiffer and
Brad Silverman with Eunice Kennedy Shriver*

*Scott Hamilton, Dr. Behrooz Behbudi, HRH Prince
Pavlos and Banessa Williams*

*Special Olympics President and CEO Timothy Shriver and
Dilek Sabanci from Turkey*

*Special Olympics South Africa athlete Daneille September,
Archbishop Desmond Tutu, and Special Olympics South
Africa athlete Elizabeth Jordan*

*Timothy Shriver, Babygirl, Dr. Nthato Motlana,
Global Messenger Ricardo Thornton, and Maria
Shriver during their visit to the Tanalani Center for
the Mentally Handicapped*

*E.T. Director Steven Spielberg celebrates with the new class of Special Olympics Global Messengers*

Attending the Special Olympics Event in 2002

With WIN-TV staff visiting the US Senate, Washington, DC

At the office of the Iranian journalist Dr. Ali Reza Nourizadeh, London 2011

Attending an interview with WIN-TV

Recording a program for WIN-TV, Jerusalem, 2010

Meeting with Danny Ayalon, Deputy Foreign Minister of Israel in 2010

At the Conference of the Women's International Organisation, Jerusalem, 2010

At the home of the late Prime Minister of Pakistan Benazir Bhutto and her husband together with my son Noah

In a meeting with the directors of Israeli 'SMART' research centre - 2011